Creative
SCRAPBOOKING

THUNDER BAY
P·R·E·S·S

CONTENTS

CREATIVE
SCRAPBOOKING

Scrapbookers who have a solid grasp of basic techniques, tools and materials will now be ready to take the next step on their creative journey. Armed with confidence, plenty of imagination and this inspirational guide to creative scrapbooking, you will soon be producing dazzlingly original and artistic layouts, embellishments and journalling.

NEW FRONTIERS

Your first scrapbook layouts taught you the essential elements of scrapbooking: balance, colour choice, title selection and embellishment. However, there comes a time when your imagination dares you to move beyond the boundaries of your early scrapbook pages, to create work for your albums that is more than mere design—it is art.

Scrapbookers who have been practising the craft for some time take a different view of their creativity. They look at photographs differently, seeing an unusual angle, a creative crop, or a surreal pattern in an ordinary picture. They look at materials differently, preparing to put paper, fabric, metals, plastic and glass to uses for which they were never originally intended—perhaps even ignoring the acid-free imperative to include a beautiful background or textured material in a layout. They look

at design differently, creating asymmetric layouts to shock and delight the eye, juxtaposing colour, form and texture. They even look at journalling differently, often allowing the pictures and embellishments to tell the story rather than relying on words to describe it.

The purpose of scrapbooking remains unchanged: a scrapbook album is a means of preserving the stories and images that will otherwise be lost to memory. Sometimes the scrapbook page is designed to help the maker recall the details of the events; other pages are designed to transmit thoughts and feelings to those who come after, speaking to children and unborn grandchildren or great-grandchildren.

All elements of a layout work together to tell a story: the choice of photograph, capturing a moment in time; the layout colour, design and embellishments, capturing the mood of the moment; and

the journalling and title, filling the visual blanks with descriptions and details of what was happening, when and where.

Turning these practical purposes into a work of creative art is the aim of scrapbooking for those whose skills are well and truly honed. The basic principles still apply, but where you take them from here is up to your imagination.

WHAT IS CREATIVE SCRAPBOOKING?

The scrapbooking techniques in this book are more advanced than the basic skills you learned as a beginner. They offer excitement and creative opportunity as you expand your repertoire of skills (and your toolkit). The range of techniques, materials and tools presented in this book will add another dimension to your crafting life and open up exciting new possibilities for the already proficient scrapbooker.

EXTEND YOUR SKILLS

The step-by-step photographs in this fully illustrated guide to creative scrapbooking are designed to help you meet new challenges with confidence. By following the instructions in this book you will develop the skills and confidence to produce elaborate and increasingly adventurous albums.

You will also be equipped to explore other avenues of papercraft, from creating elegant gift tags and cards to branching out into new areas of craft such as altered books. You will learn how to expand and make the best use of your existing kit of tools, products and materials.

NEW WAYS WITH TOOLS AND MATERIALS

You will learn how to use a variety of media–beyond paper and cardstock. It is time to be more experimental with the way you use paper. Discover how to include a range of non-paper materials in your layouts: metal, polypropylene plastic, fabric and even organic materials and ephemera. Learn new techniques for manipulating these materials and putting them to innovative uses on a page.

There are no limits to the sorts of embellishments and textures that you can use in scrapbooking: wet and dry embossing, artists' media and acrylic paints and recycled material such as waste compact discs and ephemera.

INNOVATIVE FORMATS AND STYLES

Projects and examples of creative techniques by leading scrapbooking teachers include instructions for making frames and spirellas, creating three-dimensional serendipity squares and assembling artistic collages and multilayered pages.

You can now move beyond the standard scrapbooking album to create cards, memory boxes and mini albums in an infinite variety of formats that are not dependent on the classic square or rectangular album page.

Learn how to bind and decorate your own mini album for a totally unique scrapbooking treasure. Create works of art that will grace the walls of your home with memories, rather than be hidden away in a scrapbook album in a bookshelf. Work on cardstock or canvas and make your own frame or have one custom made.

Whether you are looking to scraplift entire page designs as you experiment with new techniques, or you want to try a new tool or skill to get an effect you have in mind for your own original design, the experienced artists who have contributed their work to this book are happy to share their creations with you.

REVISITING BASIC SKILLS

Since first beginning to create scrapbook pages, you will have learnt many new skills in photography, design and papercrafts. These skills will form the basis for the adventures in creativity and imagination presented in this book. We start with a review of some of the basic scrapbooking skills that you will use for creating the projects in this book.

FRAMING PHOTOGRAPHS

A scrapbooker should be on the lookout for the best possible framing of a photograph from the time the camera is pointed at the subject. Select a viewpoint and highlight graphic elements or colours in the frame: try to compose the shot before you press the shutter.

Remember the three elements of a photograph: foreground, subject and background. Where is the subject located? Use objects, colours and shapes in the foreground and background to make a frame around the subject or to direct the attention to it.

Try to make either the foreground or the background take up a larger area of the image; for example, by having the horizon low and the subject silhouetted against the background, or by standing above the subject and having them in the foreground with the horizon at the top of the image or even out of shot.

CROPPING PHOTOGRAPHS

Naturally, not every photograph you take will be perfect. If you are snapping pictures at a party or family gathering, there is no time to compose a plain background or find a graphic angle. Sometimes you will use someone else's photographs in your scrapbook page. In these cases, cropping can make the difference between an interesting photograph and a great image.

Professional photographers use pairs of black right-angled corners made of heavy card, called 'croppers'. You can use the pairs of croppers provided in the templates section at the back of the book. By moving the corners closer together, as in the photograph above, you can try out different cropping of an image. When you are happy with the image, mark the corner points with a stylus or sharp pencil and crop by joining up the points with your paper trimmer.

MATTING PHOTOGRAPHS

Traditional scrapbook photograph mats are cut to show a narrow border of colour around a photograph on a scrapbook page. Single or double mats are standard but, by the time you have been creating scrapbooks for a little while, you'll find that you're willing to try variations on the tradition.

Use multiple mats of various thicknesses; try torn edges rather than straight ones; or cut a mat and mount the photograph off-centre. Not using a mat at all is an option. Add a textured or smudged border in a photo–editing computer program before you print out the image. Use abrasive paper to scratch a frame into the glossy photographic paper, or dab on ink to highlight the edges of the image. Draw a freehand line on the background cardstock around the photograph to create a casual frame.

MANIPULATING CARDSTOCK

Cardstock and paper, the basic construction materials of a scrapbooking page, can be treated in a variety of creative ways. These include scrunching, tearing, sanding, stitching, embossing, painting and printing. You may already have used some of these paper-manipulation techniques in your previous scrapbook layouts.

MANIPULATING CARDSTOCK

Basic textured cardstock can be altered in a number of ways to make a unique background for your scrapbook page, mat for your photographs or block for your journalling. Simple ways to change the texture of cardstock include scrunching, sanding with abrasive paper and adding corrugations with a roller. Embossing patterns and shapes with a stylus and stencil is another method you can use. Use a stylus to emboss freehand straight or curved lines into the cardstock. Use a firm rubber foam mat such as a computer mouse mat or a thick paperback book such as a telephone directory as a base for embossing. These techniques can be used on entire sheets of cardstock or on small pieces for specific purposes.

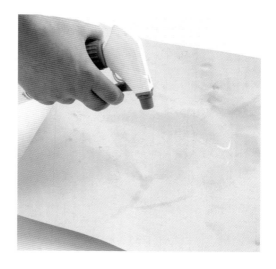

1 Wetting and scrunching cardstock adds texture to smooth sheets. Begin by wetting the cardstock thoroughly with a spray bottle or simply by sandwiching the cardstock between wet cloths and pressing down on it with your hands.

2 When the cardstock is wet, use your hands to screw it up into a ball. The tighter you squeeze the ball, the finer the network of creases and lines in the finished result.

3 Use an iron to press the cardstock flat again and remove most of the moisture. If you plan to tear the card, it can be easier to tear while it is still damp. Allow the cardstock to dry completely before using it on your layouts.

PAINTING ON PAPER

Create individual backgrounds for your scrapbook layouts by applying colour to plain cardstock using a variety of methods. Acrylic paint is the easiest form of colour to apply; use brushes or other applicators to create different effects.

Because acrylic paint is water-based, the consistency can be changed by adding artists' media. To thin paint, for example, add flow medium. To keep a thick consistency but dilute the colour, add gel medium. Apply paint using standard paintbrushes: for a roughly weathered look, apply unthinned acrylic paint with a wide-bristled brush. For a smoother texture, use a flat, bristled brush and thin paint. Use a round stencil brush to dab paint through stencils or simply in a random pattern—or try applying the paint through an open-weave fabric such as muslin or gauze. Use a sea sponge to create a mottled effect—scrunched up paper, fabric and plastic film also produce interesting textures.

Acrylic paint is inexpensive so don't hesitate to experiment with a range of applicators and thinners or thickeners—you will be amazed at the artistic effects that can be achieved.

PRINTING ON PAPER

Using dyers' pigments to colour paper can reward the adventurous with brilliant results. Dip plain cardstock into dye created with special pigments or made from household substances–crepe paper boiled in water makes a good dye that can be used as a dip or painted onto the cardstock to create patterns.

Take a leaf out of the dyers' book and try resist effects by applying repositionable adhesive, painting over the entire surface with surface pigment such as acrylic paint or even archival ink, then removing the adhesive to reveal gaps in the colour.

For fun, use the shaving-foam printing technique shown in the steps below. This method works with cardstock, paper and fabric too, and one application of pigment to the shaving foam can be reused several times, depending on the amount of dye absorbed by the material.

ABSTRACT DESIGNS

Brilliant silk dyes swirled with a wooden skewer form wonderful abstract patterns in a tray of shaving foam, pictured above. The pigments sit on top of the foam bubbles and can be simply transferred to paper or fabric using the method illustrated in the step-by-step photographs on this page.

1 Squirt a thick layer of shaving foam onto a flat surface such as a shallow tray. Smooth the surface of the foam with your hands or a flat knife blade until it is as flat as you can get it.

2 Apply dye or ink to the surface of the shaving foam and use a wooden skewer to swirl the colour around the foam, keeping it on the surface of the bubbles.

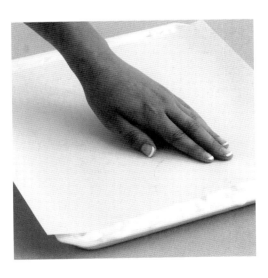

3 Carefully lay the cardstock or paper on top of the shaving foam and smooth it down gently so that full contact is made with the ink. Lift the paper away and blot with an absorbent paper towel after the ink is dry. Set the colour with a heat tool or iron according to the manufacturer's instructions.

SEWING BY HAND OR MACHINE

Stitching can be used to great effect on scrapbook layouts, either as a general decoration or as a method of fastening elements to a page. You can purchase paper and cardstock with an all-over stitching pattern either printed on the paper or pre-stitched. You can also use simple embroidery stitches or a sewing machine to create your own designs.

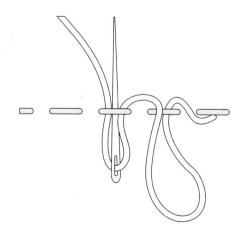

SEWING BY HAND

Stitching by hand allows you to use a wider variety of threads and to stitch through many different materials and thicknesses. Use a fine awl to pierce the holes for your stitching before passing the thread through with a large paper needle. Running stitch, back stitch and cross stitch are simple favourites, although the more adventurous stitcher might like to try fly stitch, whipped back stitch, French knots and other fancy embroidery stitches, following the diagrams below.

SEWING BY MACHINE

Set the machine stitch length to a long, straight stitch (about 5 mm or $1/8$–$1/4$ in). Feed the paper through the sewing machine slowly. Keep the tension loose so that the stitching doesn't become a row of perforations that enable the paper to tear easily.

If you have a sewing machine that does a variety of stitches you can experiment with zigzag and other fancy stitch settings to create different designs.

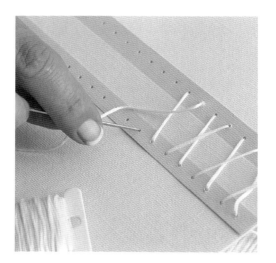
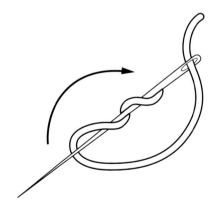
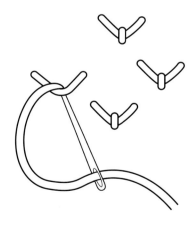

WHIPPED BACK STITCH

Work a second thread, preferably in a different colour or texture, over a row of ordinary back stitch. The needle and thread do not pass through the cardstock, they go under and over the back stitches only. Passing the needle under the stitch backwards (eye first) avoids accidentally splitting the thread.

FRENCH KNOT

Bring a needle and thread to the front of the cardstock. Wrap the thread around the needle a few times. Pass the needle back through the same hole, holding the wrapped thread with your thumb. Pull the thread gently through to the back, but not too firmly or the knot will pull through the hole as well.

FLY STITCH

Punch three holes in a triangle shape for each stitch. Bring the needle up through one hole and down through an adjacent one. Before you pull the thread tight, bring the needle up through the remaining hole, pass it around the loop of thread, then back down through the same hole.

REVISITING BASIC TOOLS

The tools you need to put a scrapbook page together are put to different uses as your skill in using them increases and your imagination invents new creative techniques. Make sure that your toolkit is well-stocked with supplies of different types of acid-free adhesives, sharp cutters and a variety of pens, stickers, stamps and ink, acrylic paints and applicators.

CUTTING TOOLS

A paper trimmer is an essential scrapbooking tool, and one that accepts up to the standard 30.5 cm (12 inch) square cardstock and paper is preferable. A trimmer with an interchangeable rotary blade is ideal: blades for scallops, pinking, deckle and other decorative edges are available as well as scoring wheels if you want to fold cardstock for mini books, envelopes or cards.

As well as a large paper trimmer, a sharp, pointed pair of paper scissors is useful for smaller tasks and fine work. Choose a lightweight pair with comfortable handles and a sharp point for getting into tight corners, and make sure they are only used for cutting paper.

Novelty paper scissors with patterned blades are useful for cutting fancy edges on cardstock and paper. Like rotary blades, these scissors are used for cutting scallops, pinking, deckle, fringes and other designs.

For cutting out lettering and other intricate shapes, a craft knife or scalpel is invaluable. You will also need a self-healing cutting mat and a metal ruler for marking and cutting straight lines. Scalpels should be extremely sharp for accurate cutting, so replace the blade regularly and keep it covered with a protective sheath when not in use.

ADHESIVES

Acid-free adhesive for your scrapbook comes in such a variety of forms that there is sure to be a suitable adhesive for any material you want to stick to your page. The simplest to use is roll-on adhesive that comes on a paper roll in a plastic dispenser. You simply guide the dispenser wheel across the paper in the place you want the adhesive and the permanent or repositionable adhesive remains on the page.

Double-sided adhesive tape comes on an ordinary tape roll or as a roll of pre-cut squares in a dispenser (photo tabs) that can be peeled off and positioned individually. These forms of adhesive are stronger than roll-on adhesive and are most useful for flat, straight surfaces.

To add dimension to a scrapbook page, you can use glue dots, which are globules of adhesive that come in a number of different thicknesses on a paper roll or sheet, or double-sided adhesive foam shapes and tape. These allow the cardstock, paper or embellishments to sit up above the surface of the page.

For metal embellishments and other odd shapes, acid-free liquid adhesive can be applied to a surface of any shape and gives extra strength if only a few points of adhesion are available.

JOURNALLING TOOLS

By the time you have been scrapbooking for some time you will have become more comfortable with writing down thoughts and feelings that make up the journalling on your scrapbook pages. You will have discovered that there are several ways of recording journalling, other than writing it with your own hand in acid-free ink.

Many scrapbookers like to use their computer to write journalling. Using a word processing program has the advantage of making the planning easy: you type in the words that you want to use, then choose a font you like in a size that fits the space available. If you are planning to write your journalling in pen you'll need to write one or several drafts to ensure the words fit and that there are no mistakes in the text.

Another means of recording journalling is to use alphabet stamps: this method is time-consuming for long sections of text but the choice of stamps can add to the feel of the page. A date stamp is useful; even if you don't use it as part of your journalling you can stamp the date of creation on the back of the layout for future reference.

Stickers, comprising words and phrases or simply letters of the alphabet, can also be used in journalling. Interspersing stickers and stamps with handwritten or computer-printed journalling places extra emphasis on selected words and phrases in the text, which looks fun and effective.

PAINT AND OTHER MEDIA

Using acrylic paints on paper and cardstock can give a variety of results. From watercolours to poster paints, you can paint abstract designs, add colour washes, paint embellishments (even metal or leather) to match your colour scheme and create patterns on plain backgrounds.

Inks, paints and dyes can also be used to alter the colour of paper, cardstock and embellishments. Walnut ink, which comes in a powder form, can be mixed with water and applied to add the appearance of age to paper and cardstock, while inks from pads can be brushed over cardstock or paper with a smudging brush or direct from the ink pad. Gesso (white acrylic undercoat) can be used to give a weathered, whitewashed appearance to many different surfaces.

Chalk is another useful colourant, available in a rainbow of colours. It can be applied using your finger, a sponge brush such as a sponge-tipped applicator, or a fine paintbrush. Applied judiciously around the edges of cardstock, it visually softens straight edges and gives body to torn paper or card.

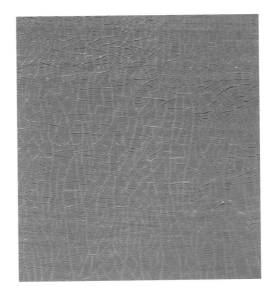

STAMPS AND INK

Decorative stamps used with the multitude of acid-free or archival ink colours that are available have a wide range of applications, from decorative backgrounds to heat-embossed accents. Stamps, especially the range of newer and larger foam stamps, can be used with acrylic paint as well as ink, embossing fluid and many other media.

Stamps range from sets of alphanumeric characters (in various sizes and styles) to words, phrases, poems and even whole sections of text designed to be used as a background for other embellishments and other stamps. Images on stamps range from simple shapes such as leaves, hearts and shells to complex pictures with lots of intricate detail.

Generic images such as leaves, flowers and shells are useful items to have in your scrapbooking toolkit. They can be used to create repetitive backgrounds by stamping multiple times over an area of cardstock; or they can be used once to embellish and highlight a particular part of the layout.

More specific images, such as detailed picture stamps or stamps with specific themes, should be bought as required and if you feel that you will get value for your money.

Experiment with rubber and foam stamps and different types of paint and ink to create unique looks for your scrapbook pages. Apply coloured ink with a brush to specific areas of a detailed stamp, or add colour to a monochrome stamped image using acrylic paints once the ink has dried.

Use embossing fluid or pigment ink with embossing powders or ultra-thick embossing enamel crystals to turn flat stamped designs into three-dimensional embellishments. A heat tool is essential for best results with embossing.

EYELETS, BRADS AND CHARMS

These small metal embellishments can serve the dual purpose of being a decorative way of securing other design elements to the page, or they can be included for their own sake. Eyelets are decorative metal rings with a shaft that passes through a hole in the page and is flattened out on the reverse side by a punch. You will need a small hammer, an appropriately sized hole punch and an appropriately sized eyelet punch to flatten out the shaft of the eyelet into a flange on the reverse of the cardstock. Nailheads work in the same way as eyelets but have a flat head on the front surface rather than maintaining a hole in the centre.

Brads are decorative split pins that come in many shapes and sizes. The sharp points push easily through most weights of paper or cardstock; the two arms of the split pin are then opened out in opposite directions to secure the brad in place. This type of fastening allows two pieces of cardstock to move independently so it is useful for securing tags and mini books that you want to turn or move in place on the page.

Metal charms can be glued, attached with eyelets or brads or tied to the page. These charms take many forms, from generic shapes such as leaves and bells to specific motifs such as baby's rattles and wedding rings.

Alphanumeric characters, words—and even phrases or short poems—are among the multitude of metal charms available from your scrapbooking supply store.

FABRIC AND FIBRES

Fabric can be fixed to cardstock directly, but it is more effective to use an iron-on fabric stiffener on the reverse side of the fabric before cutting the shape you want and gluing it to your scrapbook page. The iron-on stiffener will help prevent fraying as well as ensuring that the fabric holds the desired shape on the layout.

Fabric can be glued or stitched onto the background cardstock, or even anchored with eyelets and brads or staples.

Fibres of any type can be used on scrapbook pages. Wool, cotton and synthetic yarns are suitable for stitching or to use as tassels for tags. The more elaborately textured fibres are difficult to stitch with but you can glue them to the cardstock in a variety of patterns and shapes, couch them (stitch them down) in place with finer thread, or thread them through eyelets and around embellishments.

Ribbons and braids make great borders and decorations, and can be stamped with words or images as well as painted and embellished in other ways. Narrow ribbons can be used like fibres—tied around brads, passed through eyelets or simply glued into place to add depth to the page design. Wide ribbons and braids can be glued flat to the page or tied into large bows for three-dimensional impact.

Don't overlook workaday fibres such as household string and cotton rope to add a rustic feel. Florists' wire and fine hemp rope are great for tying and hanging other elements such as beads and charms.

SPECIAL EQUIPMENT

Tools and materials for specific purposes may not have been in your budget as a beginner, but as your skills improve and your output increases, you may find that you have uses for some of the more expensive and purpose-built tools of the scrapbooker's kit. Consider how often you will use these machines and materials before you spend your money.

DIECUTS

Many scrapbook stores have diecut machines that can be used for creating titles and novelty shapes for scrapbook pages. These machines are expensive but can be purchased for home use. The Zip'eMate personal diecut machine by AccuCut® is a simple alternative and is affordable for a scrapbooker who plans on using diecuts on many pages over several years.

Dies are metal plates with a raised impression of a shape such as a leaf or label plate, pictured top right. Alphanumeric dies and many other shapes are also available. The die is placed on a platform block, the material to be cut is placed on top and a Perspex cutting mat is placed over the top. The Perspex mat allows the cardstock or other material to be seen to ensure that the whole die area is covered.

This sandwich of materials is placed in the diecut machine, feeding the leading edge of the mats between two rollers. When you turn the handle of the diecut machine the sandwich is forced together by the rollers and the raised metal die cuts through the cardstock or paper like a biscuit cutter. On the other side of the machine the sandwich is disassembled and the diecut shape is ready.

A soft embossing mat of foam rubber and a slightly thinner Perspex mat can be used with the same dies to create embossed shapes rather than diecuts.

HEAT EMBOSSING

Take stamping one step further with the use of embossing fluid or pigment inks and embossing powder, melted with gentle heat and allowed to set. Embossing fluid is clear or almost colourless and can be applied using an ink pad or a felt-tipped applicator. When using embossing fluid the colour of the embossing powder or crystals will be the main colour of the design. When using pigment inks, the colour of the ink is incorporated into the finished result along with the colour of the powder. If you are using ultra-thick embossing enamel (UTEE), the ink colour is largely irrelevant as the embossing enamel completely covers the adhesive you have used underneath.

After stamping or even painting the cardstock with embossing fluid or pigment ink, sprinkle a generous amount of embossing powder or UTEE crystals over the entire design area. Tap the sides of the cardstock gently to ensure that every part of the fluid or ink is covered, then gently shake off the loose powder into a container so that it can be reused.

Apply gentle heat with a recommended heat tool like the one pictured at bottom left. A hairdryer is not an effective heat tool as it simply blows hot air rather than radiating heat. Be careful not to hold the tool in one spot for too long as it may scorch the paper: as soon as all the crystals are melted, remove the heat tool and allow the embossing liquid to cool and set.

OTHER USEFUL TOOLS AND MATERIALS

- Alphanumeric stencils and templates (some are included at the back of this book)
- Photo scanner, digital camera and image-editing software for your home computer
- Calligraphy pens and specialist acid-free writers
- Brayer (small papercraft roller)
- Texturizing rollers
- Shape-cutting templates and tools (some are included at the back of this book)
- Acid-neutralizing spray
- Xyron® adhesive and laminating machine
- Acid-free metal glue
- Novelty computer fonts and archival-quality printer inks
- Foam-core board
- Flower press and dryer
- Small power drill, such as a pin drill

GOLD AND SILVER LEAF

Gold and silver leaf are very thin sheets of valuable metal that must be handled with great care as they tear very easily. These types of metal leaf are usually applied all over a painted surface to give the effect of precious metal. The leaf is then covered with a clear finish to protect the metal.

In a scrapbooking layout, gold and silver leaf can be applied directly onto cardstock to give the appearance of precious metal. The leaf covering may then be sprayed or carefully painted with a fixative sealant. Small pieces of torn metal leaf can also be spread randomly over a background, or embedded in clear liquid polyurethane that hardens to form a glassy finish.

Metal charms and embellishments can be further accentuated with gold leaf, and it works really well when used under a printed transparency to highlight words or parts of the transparent image.

To apply metal leaf, spread a light adhesive over the area that you want to cover. Use a soft, fine paintbrush or your fingers (in cotton gloves) to gently lay down the leaf. Work on small areas at a time and don't worry if the leaf tears as the joins will not be visible when you have finished. Use very light pressure, as a heavy hand will cause the leaf to tear away from the surface. Finish with a sealer and apply it by following the manufacturer's instructions.

IMAGE TRANSFER AND MANIPULATION

Repeating an image or part of an image on a page using a translucent or transparent medium emphasizes the mood or a detail of the original. You can create many different effects on a home computer, including printing on fabric, transparencies, textured paper and matt or glossy surfaces. Here are a few ways of transfering photographs to other media.

COLOUR OR BLACK AND WHITE?

Printing digital images using a home computer is the easiest way to manipulate your photographs, including switching between black and white or colour with a single touch. However, it is possible to obtain similar effects using other means. Ask at your local photographic processing store about having colour prints reproduced in black and white, and enlarged or reduced in size at the same time. Alternatively, depending on the finish you require, a photocopier can produce a similar effect.

Using a large black-and-white image, as in the project opposite, focuses the attention on the facial expression of the subject. A smaller, translucent colour image adds detail that is not apparent in the big picture, without allowing the colours in the image to dictate the design of the layout.

TRANSFERRING IMAGES

There are several ways of transferring a photograph or image from opaque paper to a transparent or translucent material. You can print a photograph directly onto a transparency using a computer printer: use the printer software to select the transparency option. You need to ensure that the transparencies you use are designed for the type of printer and ink that you have.

Another simple method of transferring a photograph is to use an adhesive plastic, such as contact laminating sheets or packing tape. This method is suitable for laser prints and toner-based photocopies as well as magazine images, and is illustrated on pages 24 and 25.

Using artists' gel medium, it is possible to create a clear, softly textured finish on an inkjet photograph, then dissolve away the paper backing to create a translucent effect, as in the project opposite.

GEL MEDIUM

Gel medium is an artist medium used to increase the transparency and brilliance of acrylic paints without altering the consistency. It is an excellent binder and can be used with powdered pigments, as well as materials such as sand and sawdust to add texture. In some circumstances, it can also be used as an adhesive. You can find gel medium in art and craft stores.

Gel medium has a translucent white consistency when wet but dries clear with a smooth satin finish, making it ideal to use for transferring photographs, particularly inkjet prints that can't be transferred using other methods. Be creative and use a brush to add swirls or stripes in the gel to create a handpainted look on the finished image. Remember, the end result need not be a perfect copy of the original.

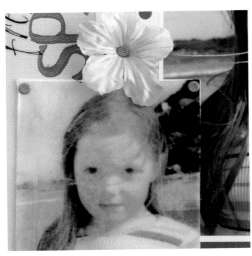

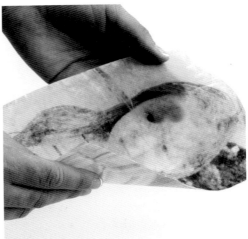

1 Choose the image you wish to transfer using gel medium. The image used in this project is a colour photograph, inkjet printed on watercolour paper. Gel medium also works with magazine images, laser prints, postcards and cards. Use the same technique as shown here.

2 Place the photograph face up. Apply one coat of gel medium evenly over the image. For a smooth finish, use an expired credit card to sweep a thin layer of medium across the photograph. You can use a foam brush or a bristle brush to add texture. When the first layer is dry, repeat the gel application five times. Allow the final coat to dry overnight.

3 Soak the photograph in warm water. Rub away the paper on the back of the image with your fingers—the wet paper should form small crumbs and start to come away. Rub carefully so that you don't damage the image on the gel. you should now have a translucent image. Allow the image to dry; place a heavy object on top if the image starts to curl.

Transferring images onto transparent or translucent materials gives more options for display as the background behind the transparency becomes part of the image. Whether the background is coloured or textured cardstock, printed paper or fabric, the image takes on a three-dimensional appearance with literally more layers of meaning.

Printing images directly onto transparencies is one way to achieve this look, but you can simply use self-adhesive plastic film, a method that achieves the same effect without requiring a computer and printer.

The tag on the left is made with an image transferred onto a piece of clear packing tape. The word 'hiver' on the tag (meaning 'winter' in French) was created with black alphabet stickers and the image—taken from a magazine photograph—was transferred onto the tape using the method shown below, then positioned on the tag. The packing tape adhesive remains strong enough to hold the image in place.

ADHESIVE PLASTIC

Various types of self-adhesive plastic film can be used to create transparent transfers from laser prints and copies as well as from magazine and newsprint pictures and text. Clear packing tape (the wide tape you use for sealing boxes and parcels) is one readily available form of adhesive plastic. The limited size of packing tape makes the transfers easy to work with and can provide interesting graphic opportunities; for example, to decorate tags. A long strip can be used as a border or, if you have a number of photographs you'd like to feature on one spread, you can assemble a comic-strip style collage on packing tape to provide a unifying treatment.

Contact laminating sheets, available from stationery stores, have a sticky surface under a removable backing that is designed to allow documents and photographs to be plastic-coated for protection without the need for a heat-laminating machine. Scrapbookers have discovered that the adhesive on contact laminating sheets fixes black laser printer and copying ink when the backing paper is gently dissolved, making wonderful transparent copies of photographs that can be used with striking effect on layouts.

The technique for dissolving the paper backing but leaving the image on the transparent plastic is similar for both of these materials. Other adhesive plastic materials may work in the same way. You can experiment with different images and with the amount of the backing paper you remove to create other transparent and translucent effects.

1 You can use small images or photographs, parts of photographs, sections of pattern or even columns of text. Simply apply the packing tape smoothly over the area of printed or photocopied material that you want to use. Trim away excess paper and tape.

2 Soak the tape strips in a shallow container of tepid water for a few minutes. The tape will curl, so turn the pieces over and flatten them out several times during the soaking process. When the paper is quite wet, you can peel away most of the paper, leaving a translucent layer of pulp and the printed image.

3 Continue to rub away the paper pulp on the back of the tape with your fingers—doing this while the tape is still soaking in the water allows the paper crumbs to float away. When all the paper has been removed, pat the tape with paper towels or a soft cloth and allow it to dry completely before using it on a layout.

full of joy

happiness

have fun

come out and play

Oscar and Byron love it when their cousins, Fletcher and Spencer, come down from Sydney for the weekend. The boys spend hours in the pool, chase each other with water pistols, build cubby houses, explore the bush with Zoe dog, ride their bikes, and have endless tug-of-war battles on their gameboys.

April 2003 – Woodlands Park

1 To transfer an image onto an adhesive laminating sheet, photocopy the photograph in black and white or print it on ordinary paper using a laser printer. Peel the backing paper off the laminate sheet and carefully place the photocopied image face down on the adhesive. Use a wooden craft stick to rub the back of the paper and ensure good adhesion all over.

2 Place the image in a shallow tray of water and allow it to soak for a few minutes. Remove it from the water and pat dry. With the plastic sheet face down, use your finger to rub the paper in small circular motions until it begins to form crumbs and come away from the plastic. Work gently in small sections and spritz with water if it becomes too dry to work. Rinse and gently pat dry.

3 Cut white cardstock squares to highlight the children's faces in the photograph and stick them to the back of the transparent image. The remaining contact adhesive should be enough to hold them in place. A light mist of spray adhesive can be used, if required. Complete the page with a line of black-and-white woven ribbon and journalling of your choice.

FABRIC AND TEXTILES

Textiles such as woven fabric, ribbon, lace and fibres enhance scrapbook layouts by adding texture, softness, colour and dimension to the page. There's no limit to the range of patterns and colours that you can use, and you can even incorporate pieces of favourite clothing or samples of furnishing and dressmaking fabrics from special places and occasions.

STIMULATING THE SENSES

Treat woven fabric as you would paper or cardstock. If you want the fabric to sit flat, it is a good idea to use a fusible web backing such as an iron-on interfacing or stiffener to help the fabric sit firm and flat on the page. Choose a fairly stiff web and follow the manufacturer's instructions for fusing before you cut the fabric to size.

Fabrics with interesting textures, such as evenweave linen, corduroy and hessian bring dimension to a flat layout. Silks and synthetic fabrics can be gathered, draped and twisted without adding too much bulk to the layout.

Ribbons and fibres of all shapes and sizes are suitable to be glued flat to the page or tied in bows or knots and left to hang. Ribbons can be used as part of the background design, or tied in strategic places to highlight features of the page.

SEWING CARDSTOCK

Most scrapbookers find that stranded embroidery cotton or rayon thread is suitable for handstitching on layouts. Use six strands together so that the large stitches are quite clearly visible. Wool is also suitable, although you may need to use a larger awl and needle to ensure that the paper will take the thicker ply.

When machine stitching, you can use an ordinary sewing machine with little or no adjustment. If the machine is also used for dressmaking or quilt piecing, it is a good idea to keep a separate needle for sewing paper and card. Practise on scraps of card and paper to select a loose tension that keeps the stitching flat, and make the stitches at least 3–4 mm (⅛ in) long so that the cardstock doesn't tear along the stitching line.

Many scrapbookers find that it is useful to purchase a small sewing machine that they keep solely for their paper crafts.

FABRIC ON A LAYOUT

Here's how to use and work with fabric in your layouts:

- use as backgrounds and mats for photographs

- create pockets for tags and journalling

- use as memorabilia (a piece of your favourite worn-out jeans, a lace handkerchief that you carried on your wedding day)

- cover compact discs or tags

- use a fabric marker to write journalling on fabric

- use iron-on backing paper to print on fabric according to the manufacturer's instructions

- transfer a photograph onto fabric and use it on a page

- create a quilt background from small pieces of fabric

- scan fabric from clothing to make matching backgrounds without damaging the garment

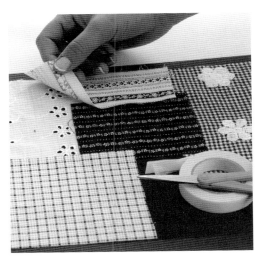

1 Select six different patterned pieces of colour-coordinated fabrics. Cut five pieces in different sizes and shapes and arrange them on a cardstock background, leaving a narrow border of cardstock around the resulting square of fabrics.

2 Use a sewing machine to stitch the edges of the fabric inside the square. A large zigzag stitch in contrasting or matching sewing thread looks great. Use the remaining fabric as a mat for the feature photograph. Position the photograph and mat on top of the stitched fabrics and stitch down the edges of the mat fabric with zigzag stitch.

3 Add decorative metal photo corners and a border of rickrack or ribbon threaded through a metal buckle along the bottom edge of the fabric mat. Place heat-resistant, double-sided adhesive tape around the edges of the fabric collage to secure them to the cardstock, then sprinkle ultra-thick embossing enamel over the tape and heat-set.

FABRIC TO PAPER

Some papers are printed with photographs of fabric designs and other textures. These can be easier to work with than the original fabrics and finishes such as painted crackle finishes, as they don't require flattening, stiffening, specific cutting tools or other special treatments.

To add dimension and texture to pages that use printed papers rather than three-dimensional fabrics and painted textures, ribbons are a neat and pretty textile embellishment. Many scrapbook supply stores sell ribbons in colour-coordinated packs just as they do papers, cardstock and other embellishments, and these can be a great source of inspiration. Stitching paper down enhances the illusion of the three-dimensional texture that is printed on it, and the addition of pretty bows does the same.

Any type of ribbon is suitable for use on a scrapbook page: woven organza and satin; jacquard designs; stitched or printed patterns; gingham; paper and mulberry paper strips; dyed silk; wire-edged; and gift-wrap ribbons.

1 Use white gesso to paint the outside edges of the cardstock: use a dry brush and bold sweeping strokes to apply the paint. Ink the edges of the cardstock to accentuate the gesso. Layer the papers and cut some pieces or tear some and roll the edges to give a variety of textures. Stitch the paper down using a machine zigzag stitch in selected places.

2 Use walnut ink and an old toothbrush to age the small tags. Lay the tags on a flat, protected surface and dip the toothbrush in the ink. Flick the bristles with your thumb to splatter ink over the tags. If the droplets are too large, blot with absorbent paper. Add journalling with an acid-free pen and tie pretty ribbons through the tags.

3 Sand the edges of the photograph using medium abrasive paper. Paint a cardstock mat in the same way as you painted the edges of the background cardstock and add machine stitching as a decorative border. Add embellishments, including the large chiffon bow and decorative photo corner.

The papers used on this page are all selected from a coordinated range of vintage-look printed patterns that mimic fabric designs and paint textures. Complementary colours (opposite each other on the colour wheel) balance each other and accentuate the neutral tones of the black-and-white photograph. A linen-textured cardstock provides a backdrop for the pretty roses and ribbons.

FUN WITH FIBRES

Narrow ribbons, fancy knitting yarns and textured embroidery threads can be threaded through eyelets and tags, wrapped around layouts and embellishments, stitched down in straight and curved lines and glued onto pages to highlight textures and shapes in a photograph. You can have lots of fun with textured yarns such as chenille, shaggy yarns and synthetic or real mohair threads.

FUSIBLE WEB

Fabric stiffener that is fused to the reverse of the fabric with an iron is useful for any fabrics that need to sit flat on a scrapbook layout. There are many different types of fusible web (iron-on stiffener) that you can use for this purpose, and most are inexpensive.

The best type is a fairly stiff interfacing that is fusible on one side only. You don't need double-sided fusible web as you will use acid-free adhesive, glue, photo tabs or double-sided adhesive tape to secure the fabric to the scrapbook page, as well as other methods of fastening.

If you choose an interfacing with a similar weight to paper you can use the stiffened fabric as you would treat paper, cutting it with scissors or a paper trimmer, inserting eyelets or brads, stapling, stitching and gluing.

FRAYED EDGES

Woven fabric tends to fray when cut. You can use frayed fabric as a feature of the page—it looks particularly good if you use coarse fabrics like hessian or linen, but can be fun with fine silks and synthetic fabrics too.

If you want a neat finished edge, there are several ways to prevent fraying. Fusible web has the advantage of preventing frayed edges if you use this type of stiffener. You can apply liquid fray stopper that you paint on with a small brush; this is useful for woven ribbons too. In an emergency, clear nail polish can be used.

Stitching down the edges of the fabric with a zigzag stitch is another way to prevent fraying. Old-fashioned hemming by hand or with a sewing machine can be done before gluing fabric to the page if you don't want to stitch through the background cardstock.

ACID-FREE FABRIC

Fabric and fibres are generally acid-free or so low in acid-causing lignin that the amount is negligible—even plant-based fibres such as hemp, linen and cotton are basically acid- and lignin-free.

Natural fibres need to be protected from the effects of the environment in the same way as paper, so an archival-quality adhesive, embellishment and storage system is still essential if you want to preserve your scrapbook album for a long period of time.

If fabric has been used or worn prior to being placed in the scrapbook it is a good idea to wash it in mild detergent before using it on a layout.

Acid-free fabric glue is available from specialty scrapbook suppliers and many craft stores.

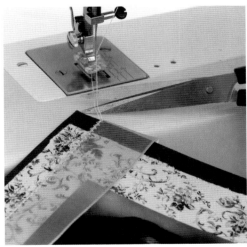

1 Choose coordinating fabrics that will give a handmade quilted look to the background of the layout. Cut them roughly to size and use a cool iron to fuse the fabric stiffener to the wrong side of the fabric, following the manufacturer's instructions. Trim the squares to the exact size you want.

2 Apply adhesive tabs to the back of the fabric squares and position them on the cardstock. The tabs will act like pins, holding the fabric in place while you stitch it down with a sewing machine. Use a zigzag stitch on the sewing machine to stitch along the joins between the squares and around the edges of the squares.

3 Attach the main photograph to the layout. Adhere the ends of the ribbon to the reverse of the cardstock and stitch the ribbon in position on the page. Print the title in reverse on pink cardstock and hand-cut with a craft knife. Ink the edges of the letters before attaching the title to the page.

SERENDIPITY SQUARES

Serendipity squares complement the theme of a page, although they are not an integral part of the journalling, title, images or memorabilia. They have a serendipitous (desirable but unplanned) association with the main elements of the page, by their colour, texture, subject or even the motifs they include. Beads, bows and charms add depth and interest.

serendipity (ser'ən dip'ə tē), *n.* a seeming gift for finding something good accidentally
(*Webster's New World College Dictionary*, Third Edition, Macmillan, 1988)

SERENDIPITY SHAPES

The simplest and most traditional serendipity square is a collage of coloured paper scraps; however, you can take these embellishments to a new creative dimension by using a variety of craft techniques. Although these decorative elements are often called serendipity squares they don't have to be square, or even rectangular–you can make them circular, triangular, polygonal, irregular or any shape you like.

Select a piece of textured card, fabric, plastic, glass or metal to be the background. Apply a finish if you like: for example, sanding, acrylic paint and crackle medium, embossed metal or card or adding ultra-thick embossing enamel.

Now search for embellishments that complement the story that your page is telling. Scout through bric-a-brac at garage sales and second-hand stores for inspiration. You need to find items that inject a sense of the moment into the layout.

1 This scrapbook page has an obvious beach theme that is complemented by the embellishments and serendipity box. Create a water-like border for the title block using metallic blue ultra-thick embossing enamel. Apply double-sided heat-resistant tape around all four edges of the panel, ensuring the ends of the tape meet closely.

2 Remove the backing from the tape to reveal the sticky surface. Pour metallic blue ultra-thick embossing enamel powder onto the tape. Heat the crystals with a heat gun until they have melted and allow the enamel to dry. You only need one layer of embossing powder to create the liquid look of the finished border.

3 Add an embossed strip to the sides of the metal letter tiles for the title in the same manner: apply a strip of double-sided heat-resistant tape, remove the backing, then sprinkle liberally with ultra-thick embossing enamel. Apply heat to melt the crystals and allow to cool.

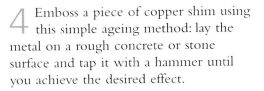

4 Emboss a piece of copper shim using this simple ageing method: lay the metal on a rough concrete or stone surface and tap it with a hammer until you achieve the desired effect.

5 Since this layout has a beach theme, the contents of the memory bottle appear to have come from the sea shore. You could collect and wash some sand from the beach, or purchase clean sand from a craft store. Add a selection of mini sequins and faux pearls to the mixture. Scoop or siphon the mix into the bottle until it is almost full. Insert the stopper with a drop or two of silicone to seal it.

6 Decorate the neck of the bottle with wire threaded with faux pearls and beads. To secure the bottle to the page, set two eyelets a short distance apart through the metal shim and into the cardstock. Thread a piece of wire through the holes, then around the neck of the bottle, and secure with adhesive tape on the reverse of the layout.

PLAYING WITH PAINT EFFECTS

Acrylic paints are useful tools for creating unusual and interesting textures and effects on scrapbook layouts. As paint is relatively inexpensive, experimenting with different methods of application can yield great results for just a little money. Begin with a selection of basic colours and branch into metallics and additives as your technique improves.

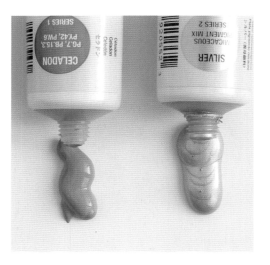

ACRYLIC PAINT

Acrylic paint is perfect for papercrafts as it is inexpensive, easy to manipulate and washes out in water. The water base in the paint will, however, cause paper and cardstock to curl slightly and lose shape, so it is preferable to use an undercoat of gesso or to apply paint sparingly.

Gesso is a professional acrylic primer used to seal surfaces such as artists' canvases before pigmented paint is applied. It provides a paintable surface on cardstock, wood, metal, canvas and ceramics.

Artists' media are additives that can be mixed with, or applied to, acrylic paint to achieve different effects. They include formulations such as gel medium, textile medium, crackle medium, flow medium and texture paste. For best results, follow the manufacturer's instructions when using artists' media with acrylic colours and you will be stunned by the effects.

BRUSHES AND SPONGES

Using a variety of paintbrushes, sponges and other applicators creates a range of textured finishes. Use wide, flat brushes to apply undiluted paint with straight brushstrokes for a smooth finish. A dry bristled brush spreads the paint roughly, while a wet brush gives a smoother application. For an ultra-slick finish, mix flow medium or glaze with the paint.

Fine, pointed brushes are used to apply paint in swirls, stripes and designs. Choose a size suitable for the feature you are painting and practise using curved strokes and wrist movements to suggest form.

Foam sponge applicators give a smooth finish, while natural sponges used with a dabbing motion add random texture.

Use your imagination when applying paint: rub with your fingertip, smear with the edge of a credit card, scrunch paper or plastic food wrap and dab.

RUBBER STAMPS

The usual way of using paint with rubber stamps is to stamp a picture or design in ink, then add acrylic paint or watercolours to colour in areas of the stamp design.

Use acrylic paint instead of ink with rubber and foam stamps. Apply paint to the raised parts of the stamp with a narrow, flat paintbrush, then stamp as usual. Sprinkle glitter or metallic paint-additive powder into the wet paint for a sparkling effect.

Another way of using stamps with paint is to paint an area of cardstock with a layer of acrylic paint, perhaps mixed with texture paste or gel medium for a thicker consistency. While the paint is still wet, stamp into it with a clean stamp to transfer the impression.

1 On one side of a transparency, such as an inkjet printer transparency or overhead projector sheet, use a paint brush to randomly apply blobs of white and pink paint. Make sure that the two colours overlap in some areas.

2 Use the paintbrush to gently blend some areas of the paint together to make areas of pale pink paint where the overlaps occur. Leave some areas pink and some totally white (not blended). You will need to work quickly before the paint dries in place.

3 Add texture by dabbing with a natural sponge. You could also use a foam sponge, a scrunched-up rag or even scrunched-up paper. When the paint is dry, turn the transparency over and attach it to the page with embroidery thread.

TEXTURE PASTE

Texture paste is an artists' medium used to create three-dimensional effects with acrylic paint. The thick white paste is easy to manipulate while wet, and retains the finish when dry. Even when dry it is very flexible and will not crack with movement. This makes it perfect for scrapbook pages that may be bent as they are turned in an album. The moisture in texture paste may cause paper or cardstock to curl up, but the dry paste is flexible so you can remove the curl when you glue it to the page.

Texture paste can be used on its own for a plain white finish or mixed with acrylic paints to produce colourful designs. While still wet, you can sprinkle it with glitter or wait until it is dry and add colour with acrylic paint or metallic rub-ons applied to the surface.

Apply texture paste to a surface with a palette knife or the edge of an expired credit card. Use long strokes, evening it out to a smooth surface for impressions of shapes or to hold embedded objects; or you can apply the paste in short, choppy strokes to give a rough effect.

APPLYING TEXTURE PASTE

● Use an old piping bag and write your title directly onto your page or to create a border.

● Use different items such as an old comb, the end of a paintbrush or a palette knife to draw lines and patterns in the surface.

● Use a lettering stencil (or brass stencil) and fill with texture paste.

● Push embellishments into the texture paste before it dries. Experiment with beads, dried flowers, charms and buttons.

● Create impressions in the surface of the wet paste using fabric, flowers or stamps; try rolling a drinking glass over the paste to create a different textured finish.

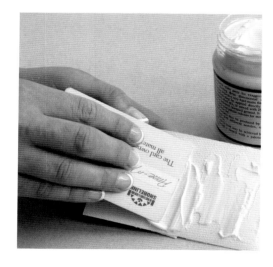

1 On canvas paper use a palette knife or the edge of an old credit card to spread the texture paste over the surface. Don't make the surface too even—use the knife or card to create texture. Allow the paste to dry.

2 Use alphabet templates to spell out a name. Apply texture paste through the template and scrape away excess paste with the palette knife or credit card before carefully removing the template. Allow each letter to dry completely before adding the next letter.

3 When all the letters are completely dry, rub metallic wax-based pigments over each letter. Attach the canvas paper to your background cardstock with double-sided adhesive tape.

4 Set aside a small amount of texture paste in a container. Add a little acrylic paint and mix thoroughly with the texture paste. Take care not to overwork the paste. Add more paint if you want a stronger colour.

5 Use a palette knife or credit card to spread the coloured texture paste over a piece of canvas paper. Smooth out the paste if you wish or leave it quite textured. At this point you can use a stylus to draw freehand designs in the pliable paste if you wish.

6 For a different effect, while the texture paste is still wet, take a foam stamp and gently push the stamp into the texture paste. Take care not to smudge the paste as you pull the stamp away. When it is dry, fix the canvas square to your background cardstock with double-sided adhesive tape.

COLLAGE COLLECTIONS

The conglomeration of intriguing ephemera that characterizes the collage style of scrapbooking looks almost as though it has been gathered up and scattered at random on the page. Far from being haphazard, the layouts on the following pages are painstakingly constructed using carefully selected embellishments to achieve a pleasing result.

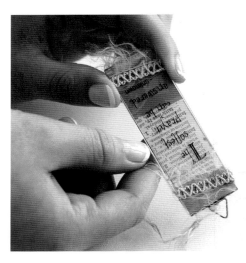

PRESENTING PHOTOGRAPHS

Photographs on collage-style layouts are rarely centred neatly on mats, so finding creative ways to attach and display photographs to the page is part of the fun of this style of scrapbooking.

Sometimes the subject of the photographs will suggest a unique method of fastening: photographs of a child on a swing are suspended from a wire line by miniature hanging clips, an echo of the suspension of a swing. In other cases, the style of the collage will supply the answer: slip a photograph behind the ribbons of a mock French noticeboard. Another solution is to simply adhere the photograph to the page unmatted—there is so much happening on the page as it is that the photograph does not need any other visual anchor.

STACKING IT UP

Collage layouts are created by assembling an inspired collection of cardstock, paper, ephemera and embellishments, then stacking the items from largest to smallest, at the same time creating balance with colour, shape and effect. It's a process of addition and subtraction, so it's wise to lay it all out before applying any permanent adhesive. Some sections of the collage may be miniature collages in themselves, requiring assembly before they are placed on the page.

There are almost no rules about what can be used on a collage layout: the three-dimensional nature of the style means that found objects and lumpy decorations are just as appropriate as flat embellishments. Alter objects such as buttons, dominoes and game pieces, tiles and tags to blend with the collage, using paint, stamps, stickers, embossing enamel and clear dimensional adhesive.

MASS OR MESS?

If you have never made a collage you might wonder how to stop a mass of embellishments from looking like a mess. One trick is to group most of the items together in one part of the page, allowing the photograph or photographs to occupy uncrowded space.

Another tip is to keep the collage elements to one main colour, plus neutrals such as black or beige. Keep scraps of fabric, ribbon and fibres in zip-lock bags according to colour and, if necessary, use ink or acrylic paints to change the colour of some embellishments to suit a particular collage.

Keep good design theory in mind and layer the collage so that your eye follows a path around the page.

little

girl

Belle

up close photo by a very patient Daddy 2004.

FOUND OBJECTS

You can use wire rig links from a fishing tackle store to provide a clothesline effect, from which you can hang photographs and embellishments using miniature metal clips. Attach the rig links to the layout using metal brads and nailheads through the loops at the end of the wire rig. As well as the miniature metal clips, use wire loops and small safety pins to attach beads, charms and tags to the wire.

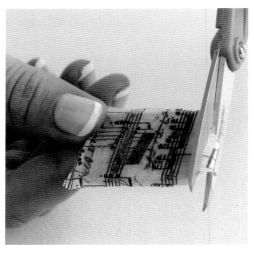

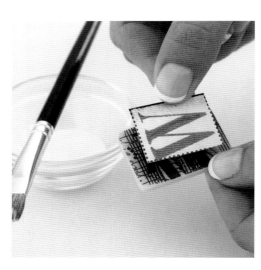

1   You can use game pieces such as letter or number tiles and dominoes to make a three-dimensional title. On the back of the game piece, apply a coat of clear-drying adhesive with a paintbrush. Smooth a piece of printed tissue paper over the adhesive and allow to dry.

2   Carefully cut away the excess tissue paper with sharp, pointed scissors, then lightly sand the edges to remove any excess paper. Apply another coat of clear-drying adhesive and allow to dry.

3   Use an alphabet sticker or letter cut-out for each game piece to spell out the words of the title. Ink around the edges of the letter before applying it to the game piece. Glue the letter to the game piece and apply a final coat of clear-drying adhesive over the top. Attach the game piece to the layout with double-sided adhesive tape or acid-free liquid adhesive.

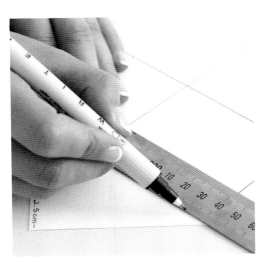

1 A French noticeboard looks elegant and it's easy to create the effect on a scrapbook layout. You can arrange photographs and other embellishments around the lattice of ribbons, tucking them underneath or pinning them in place. Start with a sheet of scrap card the same size as your background paper or card and mark out a diagonal grid of squares about 7 cm (2¾ in) wide.

2 Place the grid on top of the patterned paper or card for the background and use paperclips to hold the two layers together. Place a foam rubber mat underneath and use an awl, a large needle or a paper piercer to make small holes where the lines intersect, through both layers of card or paper.

3 Remove the card with the grid and weave the ribbons across the page, using the pierced holes as guides to where they should cross under and over. Secure the ribbon ends at the edges of the page with double-sided adhesive tape (you can cover this with a cardstock frame). Anchor the lattice by setting decorative snaps or brads into the pierced holes, pushing them through the ribbon.

1 The inspiration for this double-page layout came from a website: the artist copied the pattern of coloured squares to create a striking photo collage with personal meaning. The first step was to select images appropriate to the page's theme, which was a celebration of a long-term friendship. Turn a square paper punch upside-down to crop the images —it's easier to see what you're doing.

2 Begin laying out the collage of square photographs and select patterned papers to complement the images. Cut these into squares using the upside-down paper punch as well.

3 Create some squares from fabric and ribbon to add variety of texture to the mix. Lay double-sided adhesive tape on plain punched squares and smooth short lengths of ribbon over the tape. When the square is covered, trim the edges of the ribbon with sharp scissors.

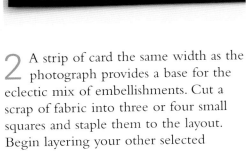

1 Make a background for the layout by layering paper, cardstock and mesh to create a flat collage in the centre of a piece of black cardstock, leaving a small border of black. The photograph has a double mat of black cardstock and patterned paper, but is offset from its mat to enhance the quirky mood of the page. A faux wax seal embellishment decorates the top left-hand corner.

2 A strip of card the same width as the photograph provides a base for the eclectic mix of embellishments. Cut a scrap of fabric into three or four small squares and staple them to the layout. Begin layering your other selected embellishments over this base.

3 Create unique elements for the collage using simple techniques like those shown in the photograph above. Stamp a metal-rimmed tag with a script image and tie on a flower charm; stamp a game piece with a detailed image; punch a hole in the centre of a small tag and attach a flower with a brad; colour metal heart and flower tags with ink and stamp with a script image.

CREATIVE JOURNALLING

Expressing your feelings is an important part of the scrapbooking process. Good journalling begins with an interesting choice of subject, enhanced by the selection of an evocative vocabulary. A large part of keeping the journalling interesting to the reader is using a format that accentuates the meaning and integrates the text into the visual appearance of the page.

CHOOSING A SUBJECT

Scrapbook pages start with one of three concepts: an event of note celebrated with words and pictures; a treasured photograph enhanced with journalling and embellishment; or an amusing or defining characteristic of a loved person.

The content of the journalling you use will depend on which of these concepts was the starting point for your layout. The basic information–time, place and people–can be supplemented with anecdotes and descriptions.

If the layout showcases a special photograph, you may journal about the way the photograph makes you feel, or be more factual about the photograph.

If you are creating a scrapbook layout to capture the personality of a loved one the journalling may focus on intimate details. If you want to keep these details to yourself, you can hide the journalling in a pocket or under a flap.

SAY IT WITH STYLE

The choice of words and the way they are written is important. While the image and embellishments of a scrapbook page contribute to the impact, the journalling can make the overall effect work harder.

Make journalling more interesting for the reader by using the present tense and an active voice. 'Your blonde curls sparkle in the sunlight' is more evocative than 'The sun was shining'.

Change ordinary words with descriptive adjectives and adverbs. 'The clowns made us laugh' might become 'The clumsy clowns make us giggle like schoolgirls'.

Use the style of dictionary definitions, recipes or the lyrics of songs to get your message across. Use quotations from poetry and literature. Write down a conversation as though it is a script for a play, or add a compact disc with the actual conversation recorded on it to the embellishments on the page.

JOURNALLING AS ART

The visual appeal of journalling is important because a scrapbook page is essentially a work of visual art. Your journalling should complement the other design elements on the page.

Handwritten journalling has its own character, and is easily formatted to fit the available space on the page. If you are journalling on a computer, font choice is paramount. Sometimes the right font will be obvious, and sometimes you will need to experiment with novelty fonts that suit the subject at hand.

When choosing a font and size, check that the text is easy to read. In general, the simpler the shapes of the letters, the easier it is to read.

Try to keep the spacing even and the lines of the same length so that the overall shape of the text block is pleasing. Avoid hyphenating words at the end of lines as this can be visually distracting.

Sweetheart

There is only the
miracle of this
moment. Savor it.
It is a gift.

Belle

11 mths

1999

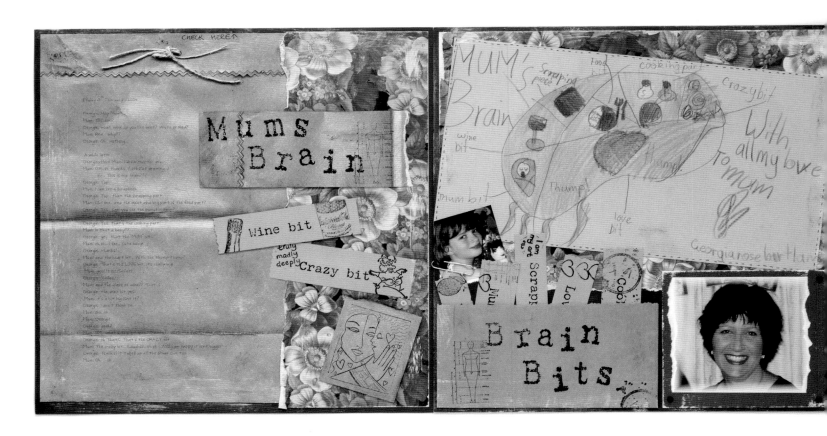

1 Using your children's artwork in a scrapbook layout is a great way of preserving these childhood treasures. Take your cue from the art and use the artist's own words as journalling. The things that children say often make amusing reading, particularly for the child herself in years to come. You can report the whole conversation as in this layout, or just use a couple of short quotes.

2 For the journalling pocket, use an plain brown paper bag, cut to size with scissors with a deckle edge. You could tear the edge or use pinking shears for a similar effect. Stamp a title on the pocket using alphabet stamps and black archival ink.

3 In the case of this drawing of 'Mum's Brain', the artist has printed on cardstock a list of the labels that appear on the original artwork and cut them into strips. The strips were then decorated with stamped images, but if you don't have suitable stamps you could use stickers and other embellishments.

POCKETS FULL OF FUN

Pockets, whether they are made from old clothing and stationery or specially constructed from fabric or paper, turn a simple page into an adventure of discovery. The fun is in delving into these receptacles and finding treasure, precious thoughts or more photographs to add further meaning to the page.

Journalling that is lengthy or of a private nature can be inserted into envelopes or pockets where only selected eyes will see it.

Memorabilia and ephemera can be slipped into pockets of fabric, vellum or paper. Add a string or ribbon that can be used to pull the item from its hiding place without damaging it or the scrapbook page.

Additional photographs that would otherwise clutter the design of the page can also be kept together in pockets, to be viewed as a supplement to the striking main image of the layout.

1 Choose a dark- and light-coloured cardstock for the background; trim the lighter colour by 1 cm (3/8 in) all around. Place the two together and use a sewing machine to zigzag stitch around the edges of the light cardstock. This stitching sets the theme of the page to match the denim fabric and other stitching that will be added later.

2 Write the title on an old stationery pocket. Trim additional photographs to fit into the pocket. Use a pocket cut with its backing fabric from an old pair of jeans and stitch it to the background cardstock using a sewing machine and zigzag stitch. Slip a decorated journalling tag inside. Decorate a kraft paper tag to look similar to the label from a pair of jeans for an authentic appeal.

3 A denim flower from a belt has been used to accent this page and visually tie the various pockets together. If you can't find a denim belt you could easily cut a similar shape from scraps of denim fabric backed with iron-on stiffener. Thread the links with ribbon, stretch the ribbon across the page and staple the ends of the ribbon at the edges.

HIDDEN JOURNALLING

There are more reasons for hiding the main bulk of the journalling from immediate view than simply recording private details that you don't want to share with others. Perhaps your journalling is very long and would take up too much room on the page. Another case might be when you plan add more information in the future; for example, after you have completed research into your family tree, or after you have shown the photograph on the page to its subject and asked for his or her recollections.

In this case you may want to create a space for hidden journalling on the scrapbook page so you can record additional information as it comes to light. Keeping it hidden means the page can be displayed in your album while it is still a work in progress.

Later additions to journalling can be added by handwriting the details into prepared spaces. You could create a mini book and add 'pages' of extra cardstock as new facts come to light, or you could leave openings behind photographs in which to slip tags or pieces of card with further details.

MULTIPLE JOURNALISTS

The person who creates the scrapbook page need not be the only person to journal on a page. Give others the opportunity to contribute their thoughts and memories to your scrapbook so it represents a whole family history.

Provide pieces of cardstock cut to size for others to write their thoughts: index cards from a stationery store are ideal for this purpose. Place the collected cards in an envelope or pocket on the page.

Save birthday cards from a milestone birthday: choose one or two to decorate the page, then create a large pocket behind the layout by adhering the side and bottom edges of a second piece of cardstock to the first with double-sided adhesive tape. Slip all of the cards with their wishes in between the two sheets.

Family vacation pages can be enlivened by having each member of the family write their holiday highlight in acid-free pen on a piece of paper or card which can then be adhered to a tag and slipped behind a photograph of that part of the vacation. Children who are too small to write their own journalling can dictate their stories to an adult.

1 Choose retro-style printed paper to coordinate with the main photograph on your page and cut it to fit as a mat under the main photograph. To echo the vintage feel of this photograph, the paper is aged by scrunching and inking with sepia ink and a stippling brush. Use your fingers to create additional creases, tears and folds around the edge of the mat.

2 Add vintage touches such as metal photo turns to hold the photo in place. Choose embellishments that complement the metal snaps used on the journalling tags.

3 The main journalling details—title, names, location, date and an evocative quotation—are printed on cardstock and cut into tag shapes. Position the title and quotation tags together with the ends aligned and use sepia ink to stamp a large vintage image over both tags. Age the tags to match the ageing of the paper and background by brushing sepia ink with a stippling brush.

LYNITA
&
KYLIE

BELLINGEN
CIRCA 1970

Sisters

WE ARE MORE THAN JUST ACQUAINTANCES
...IT'S AS IF WE ARE CUT FROM THE SAME FABRIC.
EVEN THOUGH WE APPEAR TO BE SEWN IN A DIFFERENT PATTERN,
WE HAVE A COMMON THREAD THAT WON'T BE BROKEN
BY PEOPLE OR YEARS OR DISTANCE.

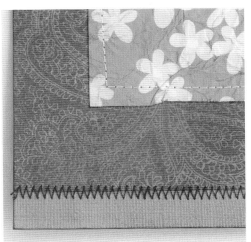

4 Create a combination of coordinated patterned paper or cardstock and age by crumpling and inking as for the photograph mat. Arrange a collage of these elements on the background cardstock and adhere in place.

5 Use machine stitching to decorate the edges of the paper pieces in the collage. A combination of coloured thread and different machine stitches adds interest to the layout and, in this case, complements the details of the hidden journalling, which talks about the girls' grandmother and their mother's memories of her dressmaking skills.

6 Embellish the tags with metal snaps and ribbons. Glue the smaller tags on the background, aligned with the edge of the cardstock. Stitch the outer edges of the tags and score close to the stitching line on the large tag so it can be folded back to reveal the additional journalling. Print the extra journalling on cardstock to match the tags, cut to fit under the large tag and glue in place.

RECYCLING EVERYDAY OBJECTS

Scrapbooks are an ideal place for recycling household items that might otherwise simply be discarded. They can be used in their original form or altered using acrylic paints, metallic wax-based pigments and other colour-changing methods. Everyday objects such as compact discs can be painted, covered with paper and fabric and even cut into different shapes.

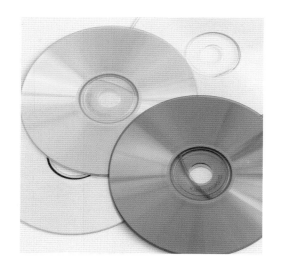

ALTERING COMPACT DISCS

Compact discs (CDs) are inexpensive and their frequent use as promotional material means that you might have some that are of no further use. There are many ways to recycle them as works of art, from hanging them in the garden to scare bird and animal pests, to using one as a coaster for your coffee cup.

To alter a CD for use on a scrapbook layout, the simplest way is to cover it with cardstock or paper that provides a plain, flat surface on which you can paint, write or add other embellishments. Use the CD as you would a tag.

A coat of acrylic paint also looks good on a CD. Sand the surface first, with coarse and then fine abrasive paper, before undercoating with gesso or acrylic primer. Then apply the paint colour or finish that you want. You can use crackle medium, texture paste or ultra-thick embossing enamel to give a glossy finish.

COVER CDS WITH FABRIC

Cover a compact disc with fabric by gluing the fabric smoothly to the front of the CD using an acid-free spray adhesive. Trim the fabric flush with the edge of the disc or, to prevent fraying, trim it about 12 mm ($\frac{1}{2}$ in) from the edge of the disc and make cuts towards the centre of the CD every 12 mm ($\frac{1}{2}$ in) all around the edge. Fold the fabric tabs to the back of the CD and add extra adhesive to secure them, if necessary. Alternatively, stitch a running stitch all around the edge of the fabric and draw it up tight to pull the fabric in behind the CD. This method adds a little bulk, which you can use in place of foam dots to help the CD sit up from the scrapbook page.

CUTTING AND PERFORATING

Compact discs are sturdy but they can be cut quite easily with household scissors, especially if you soften the disc slightly with a hairdryer or heat tool first. Score the cutting lines on the shiny side using a craft knife so the silver backing will not flake off as you cut them. Wear safety goggles at all times to protect your eyes from shards of plastic that might fly off.

Use a drill to make holes in the CD for embellishments such as brads, eyelets and fibres. Drilling small holes can also help when cutting the CD.

Cut a CD about a quarter of the way down from the top edge and add hinges to make a cover for a mini-album, as shown above (project on page 90). One half of a CD makes a great pair of wings for an angel, or a whole CD cut in half and with the sides swapped over makes a simple butterfly shape ready to decorate.

Mat the main photograph on cardstock and tie with household string to accentuate the 'mail' theme by representing a parcel.

On the Outside looking in....
Alyssa has a fascination for the mailbox. She often helps collect the mail and always hopes that there will me something for her. When she is playing outside at the front of the house she will open and shut the little door checking for mail or filling it with some toys or flowers picked from the garden. She loves the round slot for newspapers and takes delight in looking through to the other side. This day she found Dad and his camera on the other side looking back at her. MAY 2003

1 Tear the edge of a piece of printed paper and brush the torn edge with sepia ink. Glue it to a second piece of paper to create a 14 cm (5½ in) square. Using a CD as a template, cut a circle from the paper the same size as the CD. Cut a 35 mm (1½ in) hole from the centre of the circle to reveal the clear centre of the CD. Brush sepia ink around the edges and glue the paper to the CD.

2 Select postage stamps for one word of the title. Brush the edges of the stamps lightly with sepia ink and stamp one letter on each postage stamp. Glue the postage stamps, overlapping each one slightly. Complete the title using alphabet stamps, stickers or handwriting as desired. Glue a photograph behind the CD so the subject of the photograph is visible through the clear centre.

3 Make a faux CD cover by cutting a 13 cm (5¼ in) square of patterned paper. Cut a large curved section from the top edge and ink around the edges with sepia ink. Attach a smaller piece of patterned paper behind the top edge with the curved cut-out, to resemble the back wall of the CD cover. Attach the 'cover' and the altered CD to the scrapbook page.

Many household items can be used as embellishments on layouts:

- gift wrap and ribbon
- clothing labels and trim
- knitting yarn and embroidery threads
- jar and tin labels
- stamps and envelopes
- postcards and greeting cards
- old and damaged books
- doilies (paper or lace)
- costume jewellery
- silk flowers
- keys, hooks and chains
- foil lids and containers
- zippers and buttons
- paperclips and staples
- bus tickets and other ephemera
- game pieces
- bottle caps and labels
- paint colour chips and laminate samples
- keyring charms
- pieces of broken crockery
- cloth badges
- old toys
- magazines
- seed packets and plant markers
- cardboard boxes
- compact discs

CORRUGATED CARDBOARD

The common corrugated cardboard box is a boon for scrapbookers. As well as providing interesting texture it can also be used as padding to add dimension to a layout. If you are worried about the acid- and lignin-free status of the boxes you have at home, you can purchase corrugated card in a range of colours and sizes from scrapbook supply stores. Alternatively, you could spray the cardboard with neutralizing sealant either before or after it has been prepared for use and painted.

Use the corrugated card with the covering paper intact for a smooth dimensional look or peel away the outer layers to expose the corrugations and add texture to your page. You can use acrylic paint to brighten up the colour; there's a wide range of artists' media and paint finishes to choose from.

1 Select a piece of corrugated cardboard and tear it to the appropriate size and shape. Tear off the outside layer of paper to reveal the corrugations. This makes a great textured photo mat.

2 Use a dry paintbrush to roughly paint the cardboard with gesso or white acrylic paint. When this layer is dry, add a touch of lavender paint in the corners. Stick the photograph to the mat and place on the layout.

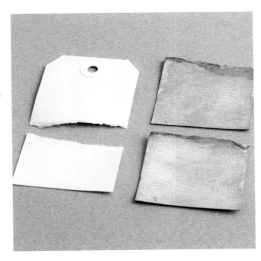

3 Age a tag to match the look of the corrugated card. Tear a manilla tag in half, then paint with walnut ink (above, top right). Once the ink is dry, use a dry brush to paint gesso or white paint roughly over the tag for a subtle effect (above, bottom right). Add journalling in acid-free pen or decorate the tag with a sticker and stitch around the side and bottom edges.

MINIATURE BOOKS

To tell a story from start to finish may take many words and several images. It doesn't matter whether the story is a chronological account of an event or a collection of evocative memories: there is the logistical difficulty of including so many words and images on one or two scrapbook pages without cluttering the design. Mini books can be the answer.

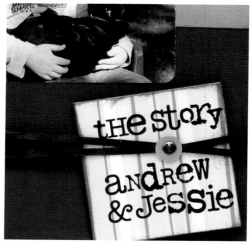

CONSTRUCTING A BOOK

There are three main ways of constructing mini books to use on scrapbook pages. The simplest is to create a book of individual leaves of cardstock or paper, cut to size and bound together along the left-hand edge with staples, stitching, eyelets and fibres or any other method. This type of book may have a self-cover or be overlaid with a slightly heavier cardstock cover. Another method of binding might be to insert eyelets in one corner of each page and hang the individual pages on a split ring.

Another easy mini book method is to cut a strip of cardstock to the height you want the book to be, then score the strip at regular intervals and fold it into a concertina shape. Attach a heavier cover to the front page (this helps to keep the concertina flat on the page).

STITCHED BOOKS

A book of paper or cardstock rectangles stitched down the middle and folded to form a booklet is another format for a mini book. For this method, cut several rectangles the same size (one for every two leaves you want in the book) then trim the inner pages level with the outer ones after the book is folded.

Use the outside leaves as the cover of a stitched book, or create a heavy card cover by gluing the outer pages of the stitched book to squares or rectangles of heavy card.

CONTENTS OF A MINI BOOK

Use your imagination when it comes to filling a mini book. You can use it to tell a detailed story about the event or person depicted on a scrapbook page.

You can use it to chronicle a period of time such as a month or year in your life. You may fill it with personal thoughts and feelings such as goals and ambitions, particularly if you don't want everyone to see your private thoughts.

A mini book may contain a series of photographs of the subject of the scrapbook page over a period of time, or you could construct it as a type of comic strip of the same person or event, like a time-lapse film!

Think of a mini book as a small version of a scrapbook album. The pages need not be all the same: some could hold images, some could contain journalling, while others may be pure embellishment.

Use a wide ribbon to create a holder for the mini book on the scrapbook page. Adhere the ribbon securely to the page at the point where the book will sit. Place the book on the ribbon and tie a big bow around it to secure it in place.

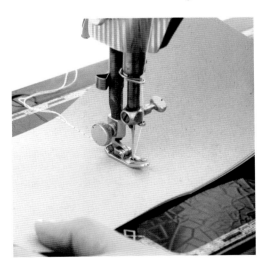

1 For an eight-leaf, saddle-stitched book, cut four pieces of kraft paper 10 x 20 cm (4 x 8 in). You will be able to cut all the pages for this book from one 30.5 x 30.5 cm (12 x 12 in) piece of cardstock. Score and fold each rectangle in half to make a 10 x 10 cm (4 x 4 in) square card.

2 Open out the folded cards and place them together with the scored folds aligned. Stitch down the scored centre line using a sewing machine, and back stitch at each end. Fold the book along the stitching line and trim the edges of the inner pages flush with the outer page, which will be the cover.

3 This mini book was intended for private journalling, so embellishment was kept to a minimum, leaving the focus on the writing and plenty of space for the journalist to express herself. Printed paper can be used to fill empty space and subtly decorate the pages. Ink the edges of the pages either before or after the journalling is written.

TAGS AND TRINKETS

Tags are the perfect medium for a mini book as they can be purchased or cut to a size just large enough for small photographs and pieces of journalling. Bind the pages of a tag booklet together through the hole punched at the top or use acid-free adhesive tape to join them into a concertina shape. Alternatively, you could stitch them together at the flat end and use the embellishments as page turners.

FOOD FOR THE SOUL

Mini books and albums are perfect for recording uplifting quotations and poems. Pairing a quote with a photograph or image gives the reader food for the eyes as well as the mind, and the act of leafing through the tiny pages is a satisfying one too.

You can transcribe the wisdom of ancient proverbs or simply jot down the sage advice from your mother in a mini book: write down the old family recipe for insect repellent or the steps in the ritual for the perfect cup of tea.

Create a mini book to describe the way your personality fits your horoscope, and decorate it with symbols of the zodiac or of the Chinese horoscope, depending on which suits your belief system. Personalize the 10 Commandments or the Six Perfections of Buddhism and record them in a mini book.

PRIVATE: KEEP OUT

Scrapbooks should contain pages about the maker as well as his or her family and friends but it can be daunting to decide what to reveal about yourself. Using a mini book to keep journalling private, or at least available only to certain readers, is one way to relieve the tension.

Use mini books on personal layouts: list all the things you like about yourself, or what you want to change. Draw up a contract of goals and ambitions, then check every so often to see whether you are meeting your own needs.

Make a time capsule about yourself: record the date and note your favourite pop song, what you ate for lunch, who you spoke to last on the telephone, what your next major shopping purchase will be, and so on.

LITTLE THINGS

Mini books are cute. It's hard to resist little toy poodles, kittens, babies, dwarfs, fairies, rosebuds and cupcakes. So turn your mini books into treasure troves of tiny embellishments and images and make them irresistible too.

Crop photographs to fit the pages of your mini book. This will encourage you to focus on the important aspects of the photograph and look for an interesting way to crop the image so that it has maximum impact. This will also force you to rid the image of distracting background elements.

Include small items that help to communicate the story, such as keys, heart motifs, pressed flowers and tiny bows. Try to keep embellishments fairly flat so you can still close the mini book comfortably.

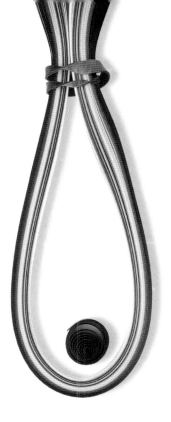

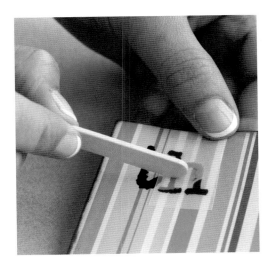

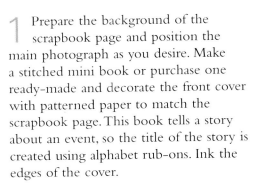

1 Prepare the background of the scrapbook page and position the main photograph as you desire. Make a stitched mini book or purchase one ready-made and decorate the front cover with patterned paper to match the scrapbook page. This book tells a story about an event, so the title of the story is created using alphabet rub-ons. Ink the edges of the cover.

2 Print journalling on shipping tags and trim them to the size of the mini book pages. Attach a small square of coloured cardstock to match the page at the top of each tag. This makes a visual reference to a normal tag top and helps keep the pages flat.

3 Attach a photograph cropped to the size of the mini book and the accompanying tag into each open spread of the mini book. Decorate with ink and small stickers. Thread strips of leather or cardstock through a metal ring or buckle and stitch the ends to the scrapbook page. Slip the mini book behind the leather straps.

METALLIC EFFECTS

Metallic finishes such as acrylic paints and additives, ultra-thick embossing enamel and dust-on or rub-on pigment finishes can add rich texture and dazzling colour to your scrapbook pages. The techniques required for these effects are easy to learn and you'll have a lot of fun coming up with new uses for them in the pages of your scrapbook.

EMBOSSING ENAMEL

Embossing is a raised design on a surface, and embossing powder or enamel is a means of raising a flat, stamped design from the page, giving a glossy metallic finish. Used with colourless embossing ink or other pigment inks, embossing powder is applied in the form of coarse or fine crystals (depending on the required result) and melted using a heat gun to bond with the ink or adhesive.

POWDER TO LIQUID

Embossing powders range from very fine granules to the coarse crystals known as ultra-thick embossing enamel. The larger the crystals, the more three-dimensional the finish when heat-set, and the longer you will need to apply heat to melt the powder. Drying time is also longer for thicker enamels, but this also gives you the opportunity to work with the liquid enamel and create interesting effects.

As well as applying ultra-thick embossing enamel to an inked or adhesive surface to create raised embossing, you can apply it to an area or shape, melt the crystals and then stamp or draw a design in the hot enamel. This results in a negative- or reverse-embossing effect.

You can also melt the crystals in a craft melting pot and use the liquid to create three-dimensional embellishments using decorative moulds.

1 Print names on a transparency so that they are a suitable size to fit underneath clear page pebbles. Print them first on plain paper to ensure the font is the right size. Glue the right side of the transparency to the underside of a clear page pebble. Trim the transparency to the edge of the pebble.

2 Cut metal tiles out of thin sheet metal or purchase ready-cut tiles from your craft store. Dust the tiles with an antistatic puff and draw a rough circle on the tile with embossing fluid using a foam applicator or a VersaMark pen. Fill in the middle of the circle with the embossing fluid.

3 Sprinkle embossing powder over the circle and shake off any excess. Heat the enamel and sprinkle on more powder while it is still hot. Continue adding powder and heating the enamel until you have a good puddle of liquid. Squash the page pebble into the enamel and leave it to cool. Repeat to make one tile for each name. Link the metal tiles with fine wire and attach them to the layout.

Bræðurnir Í Sumar Bústaðnur. 12/02

METALLIC RUB-ONS

Rub-on metallic pigments are available from most scrapbook stores; they resemble palettes of creamy eyeshadow colours. Using a fingertip or a sponge applicator, these wax-based pigments can be smeared over a surface to add a slight metallic sheen, either in a colour to match the surface or in a contrasting metallic shade.

When using your fingers to apply rub-ons, practise with a small amount on scrap paper. If you apply too much of the pigment at once you can end up with fingerprints on your work. Practise blending and swirling the pigments together in order to create interesting patterns. You can buff the colours with a soft, lint-free cloth to enhance the finish. You can use metallic powder additives to create similar effects with paint or ink.

Allow some drying time; however, if you find the pigment is still easy to remove you may need to spray it with a fixative.

DESIGN TIP

To create the torn windows on the layout opposite, tear pieces out of the cardstock, either from the side edge or in the middle of the page. Place acid-free double-sided adhesive tape around the edges of the holes on the reverse of the layout and position printed paper, vellum, ribbon or fabric over the holes. When you turn the layout back to the front, the background material will be visible through the holes.

1 Cut a frame from thick black card to surround the main picture in the layout. Use the rectangle cut from the centre, or any size rectangle you like, to make the cover of the mini book for hidden journalling on the page.

2 Use an embossing ink pad or a black archival ink pad to cover a small area of the frame, starting in one corner. Use the same technique for the mini book cover: you can prepare the two simultaneously or work on one at a time.

3 Sprinkle the newly inked area with ultra-thick embossing enamel, shake off the excess powder and apply heat with a heat gun to melt the crystals. Allow to cool. The melted embossing powder gives a slightly raised, dimpled surface that looks a bit like beaten metal.

4 Continue this process by inking small sections of the frame, sprinkling with a different-coloured powder and setting with a heat gun. Repeat for the cover of the mini book.

5 When the embossed surface is dry, ink the edges of the frame and the book cover with purple ink. Attach the frame to the layout.

6 Attach the book to the layout by placing pairs of eyelets on either side of the position for the book and threading gold elastic braid through the eyelets; secure the braid at the back of the layout.

PEARL EX

Pearl Ex gives a soft metallic finish to surfaces and is safe, non-toxic and resists tarnishing, so it is an excellent choice for archival-quality scrapbooks. Pearl Ex can be mixed into liquids such as acrylic and oil paints as well as dusted onto paper and card without the use of adhesives. To prevent mixing of colours in its dust form, it can be sprayed with fixative to allow multiple layers of metallic colour.

Pearl Ex can be mixed with polymer clay and wax or dusted onto the surface of these materials after they have set. It can be dusted onto shrink plastic before heating, so that the granules shrink into the surface as the plastic sets.

While Pearl Ex is not an embossing powder on its own, it can be mixed with clear embossing powders to achieve a metallic effect.

1 Wipe the cardstock with an antistatic puff before you begin. Ink a large background stamp with embossing ink or fluid (be careful to ink only the stamp and not the mount). An embossing fluid pen is the most effective way to apply the fluid.

2 Stamp the design in position on the cardstock. Brush chalk or Pearl Ex over the stamped design and buff with a soft cloth to remove excess powder. Keep adding Pearl Ex until you are happy with the strength of the colour.

3 If you plan to use additional layers of powder pigment as in this example, spray with a fixative before moving on to the next layer. Repeat the process with a different stamp and a contrasting colour of chalk or Pearl Ex.

Brush the edges of the treated card with embossing fluid and Pearl Ex before spraying for a final time with fixative spray. Once the fixative spray has dried you can stamp or print journalling over the top without risking damage to the metallic powder. The spray will also prevent the powder from rubbing off in the sleeves of your scrapbook album.

RETRO STYLE

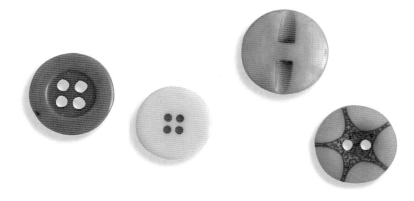

The colours, shapes and fonts that were popular in the 1960s and 1970s are experiencing a resurgence in the 21st century. The symbols and images of those groovy, swinging decades add a buzz to scrapbook layouts, celebrating both the past and the present. Use novelty fonts and graphic shapes with bright, hip colours to recreate the funky style of these eras.

RETRO COLOUR

Whether or not you were alive in the '60s and '70s (and whether or not you are old enough to remember), you will recognize the colours that were typical of the period: hot pink, lime green, bright orange and yellow, chocolate brown.

White was very chic—white dresses, white boots, white lips, white eyelashes, white accessories. This was partly a question of style, with the white serving as a blank canvas to contrast with and emphasize the bold, bright colours. But it was also a question of practicality in clothing: new easy-to-clean fabrics, as well as new mechanical washing machines to care for them, became affordable and popular.

In the home, the development of plastic and fibreglass moulded furniture, sturdy and easy to clean, also did away with the need to have dark, muddy upholstery fabrics that would 'hide the dirt'.

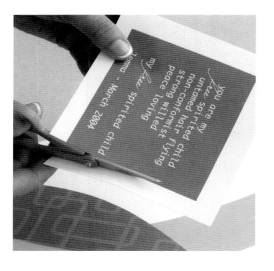

1 Create the title and journalling using differing text sizes and print in colours to complement the papers you have selected for a retro look. Place the journalling in a text box and use your computer word-processor tools to change the text to white and the background to orange. Print on photographic paper for a glossy finish.

2 Using a paper punch with various-sized punch heads, create the wavy border across the bottom of the cardstock. Work two small holes, three medium, then three large, then three medium and continue repeating this pattern in waves across the page. Turn the cardstock over and lay small squares of coloured card behind the holes to show through on the front.

3 Punch or cut basic flower shapes from white cardstock and select buttons in funky colours to match the retro paper designs. Ink the edges of the flower petals to give them a more three-dimensional look. Stick a button to the centre of each flower, then stick the flowers to the page.

you are my
free spirited child
untamed hair flying
non-conformist
strong willed
peace loving

my *free* spirited child

free spirit

RETRO SHAPES

Life in the '60s and '70s was a rollercoaster and shapes were smooth and curvaceous rather than rigid and square. From the hi-tech organic shapes of moulded furniture to the psychedelic waves of Marimekko fabric prints, straight lines were out of fashion.

In scrapbook pages, create organic curves by using corner-rounding punches on photographs, mats, journalling blocks and even on the background cardstock itself. Wrap waves of colour across the layout by cutting curved strips of brightly coloured paper. Printed papers with retro spots and stripes complement stylized flowers, bringing to mind the 'Flower Power' movement of the '60s.

VINTAGE AND RETRO FONTS

Lettering that matches the style of a retro page is easy to find. There are fonts that are specifically designed to look like the kind of lettering that was popular in the decades of the '60s and '70s.

Sans serif letters with rounded edges give a retro feel. Then there are the fonts that resemble the manufacturer's emblem from a Cadillac or a juke box, the cover of the menu from a drive-through café, or the title of a vintage magazine. There are fonts available that mimic the plastic labelling machines that were popular for putting names on everything from overcoats to school books, and fonts that have psychedelic curls and stars incorporated into the letters.

Going even further back, fonts for vintage layouts emulate the type of copperplate handwriting that was taught in early 20th century schools, while formal calligraphic script echoes the romance of the Victorian era of the 19th century and before.

A basic selection of fonts is included with most computer word-processing software, but more specific fonts are available online. Some font websites offer fonts for free, as shareware, or allow you to download incomplete character sets as test samples. Other websites sell fonts for personal use, which are often quite inexpensive. These fonts can be used on most computers and printed out for your scrapbook layouts.

METALS AND MINERALS

Incorporating metals and minerals such as mica, shim, gold leaf, metal tiles and even glass into your scrapbook pages allows you to create interesting effects on your layouts. Some of these materials require special tools and careful attention, while others are easy to work with using tools you already own.

METAL

Using metal on a scrapbook layout is hardly unusual, as this material features in many embellishments from eyelets and brads to staples, wire and metallic paper. Using thin metal sheets, such as copper, brass or aluminium shim, is similar to using paper or cardstock. These materials can be worked with paper scissors and trimmers; they can be punched to take eyelets or have shapes punched out of them; they can be embossed with a stylus, curled around a wooden skewer or even stitched onto the page. Shim of various thicknesses (gauge) is available in coloured finishes as well as traditional copper, brass, steel and aluminium.

Gold and silver leaf can add opulence to special layouts and, while the materials can be expensive, they can be used judiciously to create wonderful effects. Apply metal leaf directly onto cardstock, use it over wet ink to highlight stamped designs, or add precious metal touches to inexpensive embellishments.

MICA

Mica is a naturally occurring silicate material. It sometimes crystallizes into sheets, which can be separated into layers of different thicknesses. Mica can come in many different colours such as grey, yellow, green, red, brown or transparent.

It is photo-friendly, as it does not contain acid or lignin that will cause paper and photographs to fade and become brittle. The natural variations in colour and density add to the effect that is created on the page.

Mica sheets are available from many stockists of scrapbooking supplies.

Use mica on your scrapbook pages to create unusual effects:

- mat a photograph or create a translucent overlay to accentuate parts of the image
- stamp, emboss or gild the mica
- frame a photograph
- highlight words or an image with pieces of mica
- create faux tiles
- use a thin transparent layer in a frame or slide mount as a lightweight alternative to glass and perspex
- place ink between two layers of mica to change texture and colour
- sandwich flat items between two layers to hold them in place and preserve them.

WORKING WITH MICA

You can vary the colour intensity of mica by separating the layers. Use your fingernail to push gently on the edge of the top layer until it begins to separate. Peel the layers apart until the mica is the desired thickness. The thinner the mica sheet, the more flexible it is and the more translucent.

Mica can be cut with a paper trimmer, scissors or a knife; it can also be torn and punched with craft punches.

Attach mica as you would attach a transparency or vellum, using invisible adhesive or hiding the adhesive under other embellishments. You can be creative in the way you attach it. Mica easily accepts eyelets, brads, staples, conchos, safety pins and other fastening embellishments.

Stamp, gild and emboss mica as you would other smooth materials such as a transparency. Be sure to allow sufficient drying time for the ink. While mica will not burn or melt, it may be discoloured by too much heat.

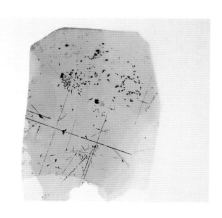

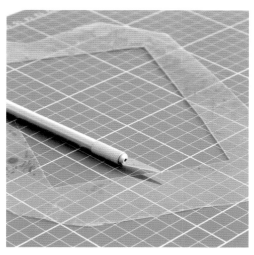

1 Choose a piece of mica to make your frame. An irregular shape creates a pleasing effect. Tear the outer edge of the mica to create the desired shape, if necessary. You will find that the sheets of mica can be easily separated by slipping a fingernail between the layers and gently peeling them apart.

2 Use acid-free ink or pens to add extra colour to the mica. You can sandwich ink between layers and move the layers around to blur the still-wet ink. Place a photograph under the mica, then use a pen to mark a point on the photograph just inside each corner. These points will be your cutting guides.

3 Use a craft knife and ruler to cut out the centre of the frame. If you feel confident, cutting freehand gives a looser, more natural effect as the lines are not perfectly straight. Glue the photograph to the background and fasten the mica frame over the top.

PAINTED METAL

Metal embellishments can be painted and decorated to suit a scrapbook page. It is important when decorating metal to remember that it has a smooth surface that will not absorb water. This means that acrylic paint won't adhere to the surface easily.

Small metal pieces such as brads and metal frames that won't be handled often can be painted with acrylic paint; however, if you want an opaque finish it's a good idea to paint the metal with a coat of gesso first. A light sanding with fine abrasive paper will also provide a key in the metal surface to help the paint adhere.

Metal can also be stamped or coloured with ink, although you may need to experiment with different types of ink for the best results. Some inks will not adhere to metal at all, while others may need to be set with a heat tool. All-purpose inks such as StazOn™ will usually adhere to metal.

METAL LEAF

Applying delicate sheets of precious metal to a surface is an operation that requires some skill and practice. For basic gilding (application of metal leaf) you will need a base coat, metal–leaf adhesive, metal leaf, a pair of soft cotton gloves, a soft bristle brush and a sealer coat.

To prepare the surface for metal leaf, a base coat of red paint is traditionally applied. Unless you want to leave some of the surface exposed, the colour of the base coat is not important, nor is its presence essential.

Metal leaf adhesive is normally a milky liquid that dries clear and tacky after 10 minutes. Follow the manufacturer's instructions when working with this adhesive: some recommend that you wait around an hour before applying the leaf.

Wear cotton gloves when working with metal leaf to prevent it from being contaminated with the oils from your

skin. Use your fingers and a soft bristle brush to apply small pieces of metal leaf, smoothing it with the brush as you go.

When the surface is completely covered, buff the metal with a soft cloth to remove any loose pieces and add shine. Coat the leaf with sealer to protect the surface and to prevent tarnishing.

Dolphin Discovery

Seaworld - April 2003

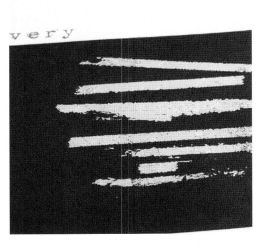

1 Using suitable adhesive for the metal leaf, swipe some strokes over the background cardstock. Allow the adhesive to dry until it is just tacky to touch, then apply the silver leaf over the adhesive. Brush away any extra metal leaf with a soft paintbrush.

2 Use a computer word-processing program to type a selection of words using differing text sizes and fonts. Make the background black and change the text to white. Reverse the image and print onto a transparency sheet. When the ink on the transparency is dry, cut out a 15 cm (6 in) diameter circle, selecting a section where the silver leaf highlights particular words.

3 Glue the transparency circle over the silver leaf and smooth with a soft cloth to ensure it lies flat. Cut a 6 cm (2¼ in) diameter circle from the transparency, centred on a key word. Use the same silver-leaf application method as before to make a single strip that highlights the main word in the smaller circle.

LAYOUTS ON COMPUTER

Some scrapbookers use computers for the basics, such as printing out journalling or titles onto cardstock and paper. Others like to edit and touch up their digital images using computer software before printing them out or having them printed professionally. A few scrapbookers go completely digital, using software to create entire scrapbook pages.

COMPUTER FONTS

Journalling and titles can be printed using the standard fonts that come with your computer word-processing software, but you can enhance the selection of specialty fonts by purchasing new ones on CD or disk or by downloading from the Internet. Type the word 'fonts' into your favourite search engine and you will see that there is a huge variety of novelty fonts available. Many are free, sometimes complete and sometimes as test samples (with some letters and characters missing). Others are available to purchase for personal use at a small cost. These fonts can then be added to your word processor's font folder and used in your scrapbook pages.

To print on cardstock or specialty paper you may need to make some adjustments to your printer, both in the dimensions of the paper and the way the ink is applied. Refer to the manufacturer's instructions to see what you can do, and be prepared to experiment a little to obtain the best results.

To print fancy lettering on cardstock to use as a cutting guide for a craft knife, you need to use the Format Font menu to select Outline character style, and then use the drawing tools to flip the text horizontally. This allows you to print the letters on the back of the cardstock so that no outlines will be visible after you have cut them out with a small pair of paper scissors or a craft knife.

PHOTO-EDITING SOFTWARE

Most digital cameras and many new computer operating systems come with basic image-editing software that allows you to adjust your photographs. Some of the basic tools can: brighten up dark images or darken overexposed images; crop photographs and straighten them; remove colour casts (if a photograph appears too blue or green for example); remove red eye (caused by the camera flash reflecting off the blood vessels in the retina); and sharpen soft focus.

Specialty image-editing programs take these tools even further and allow you to cut out background, change colours, remove unwanted parts of the image and apply filters of various textures.

You can use these programs with images from a digital camera or with scanned copies of photographic prints. Computer image scanners are readily available and reasonably inexpensive, and many new multifunction printers have scanning and copying capabilities.

Software such as Adobe Photoshop Elements and Microsoft Digital Image Pro or Ulead PhotoImpact and Apple's iPhoto are among the most common computer image-editing programs.

SCRAPBOOK LAYOUTS

Using computer software to create complete scrapbook layouts, including embellishments such as eyelets, buttons and fibres that look as though they are three-dimensional, is the method of choice for many who like the idea of being able to store their entire scrapbooking output in the space of a compact disc or DVD.

Using scanned paper, fabric and cardstock as backgrounds, or simply applying textures to coloured backgrounds, positioning photographs and adding embellishments and journalling to the files is simple once you become familiar with the software tools. Digital scrapbooking suppliers also sell CDs that include images of backgrounds, embellishments, fonts and preformatted pages to get you started.

As well as programs like Adobe Photoshop Elements and Microsoft Digital Image Pro, scrapbook-specific software is available, such as Hallmark Scrapbook Studio, Nova Art Explosion Scrapbook Factory Deluxe and Bröderbund PrintMaster.

PRINT YOUR OWN PHOTOGRAPHS

If you are printing photographs on your home computer, you can use image-editing software to add words and other special effects to the photograph. The photograph above has been given a soft-focus border and had the title added in white lettering before the photo was printed out and attached to a layout with other embellishments.

1 Open a file on your computer in your word-processing or graphics program. Most word-processing programs allow basic images to be inserted and manipulated as well as rotated and coloured. A graphics program allows even more options for manipulation.

2 Use text and picture boxes to overlay images and text. Create a text box for each element and move it around the page until you are happy with the placement. Use a brush tool to create the flower and add texture and colour. Cut and paste the flower image and change the size, shape and colour using the graphics tools.

3 Print the background on cardstock or decorative paper to use in your scrapbook layout. If you are doing the whole page digitally, save the background as a single layer and add photographs and embellishments in new layers over the background image.

SEE-THROUGH LAYERS

Using transparent materials on a scrapbook page can be a challenge. Here are some fun ideas for printing on, etching into and layering transparencies and film to create interesting effects. Almost everything can be seen through a transparent layer, so you will need to use transparent adhesive or use other methods of securing these materials to the page.

PRINTED TRANSPARENCIES

There are several types of transparency made of polypropylene, which is stable and suitable for archival-quality scrapbook pages. Transparencies printed with words or images are available in scrapbooking stores, as is vellum–which might be considered a 'translucency'.

Overhead projector sheets are totally clear and are designed to be used in computer printers–either inkjet or laser (toner-based) printers–and photocopiers. There is a difference between the type of transparency that is suitable for inkjet printers and and those designed for laser printers or copiers so take note when you are purchasing that you have selected the correct type of transparency.

If you want to apply stamps, paint or rub-ons by hand, or simply use the transparency to create a window into a shaker box or other dimensional embellishment, the type of transparency doesn't matter so much.

Transparencies for inkjet printers have a rough side and a smooth side. The rough side is the printing side. If you find the ink is forming little droplets or smudging easily, you have probably printed on the wrong side of the transparency, or used the wrong type. Don't forget to change your computer printer settings to a transparency setting.

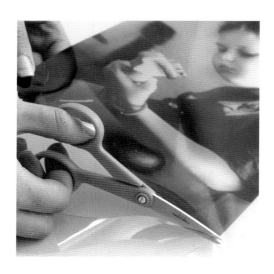

1 Print a photograph or image in black and white onto a transparency. Trim the transparency around the printed area.

2 Select a transparency preprinted with words or images to use with the photograph and trim it to highlight your choice of title and imagery. Use fine grade abrasive paper to distress the edges of the transparency and arrange the pieces on the background cardstock. Use vellum adhesive to attach the film to the background cardstock.

3 Lay the transparent photograph over the preprinted transparency and use a domestic engraving tool to etch the title into the photograph transparency where it overlaps.

You can print words on a clear transparency to create interesting layers of text and images, or you can use transparent images over text and coloured backgrounds to give a different emphasis.

TRANSPARENT PHOTOGRAPHS

Printing colour or black-and-white photographs on transparencies gives an interesting effect. You can use the transparency to create an image to overlay journalling (rather than the other way around, by creating a transparency of journalling to overlay the image).

You can layer colour images and black-and-white images of the same scene or subject as shown in the project on page 77, or cut away sections of an opaque image and use the transparent version to fill in the gaps. Placing different-coloured or textured backgrounds behind sections of a transparent image can highlight certain parts of the image, as shown in the image transfer project on page 25.

A totally transparent scrapbook page such as the example on page 76 is a radical take on the idea of transparencies in a scrapbook page. The image appears in colour on a stiff polypropylene sheet so that it can be seen from both sides. Embellishments and minimal journalling have been selected because they will be seen from both sides of the page.

ADHESIVES AND ATTACHMENTS

Because transparencies are see-through, ordinary adhesive will be visible on the finished scrapbook page unless you cover it with stickers or other embellishments. Vellum adhesive in spray or tape form is designed to be invisible under transparent and translucent materials and is a good alternative method of adhesion.

Self-adhesive transparencies that can be used in a computer printer are available, as are adhesive sheets for heatless laminating that can be used for photo transfers as shown on page 25.

Another way to solve the problem of visible fastenings is to make a feature of them. Attach transparencies with eyelets, brads, staples and stitching (use long stitches if machine stitching). Attach tiny bulldog clips to the page to hold the transparency slightly above the background cardstock for an interesting three-dimensional effect.

TRANSPARENT OR TRANSLUCENT?

Transparent material is completely see-through, like the unprinted areas of overhead projector transparencies. Transparencies suitable for scrapbooking and papercraft often have a glossy finish that needs to be taken into consideration when planning the finished appearance of your scrapbook layout.

Translucent material has some colour of its own (such as vellum) but it is possible to see through it to the colours and patterns that are behind it. This kind of transparency is great for softening harsh lines and bold colours, adding a matt, calm finish to your page.

Opaque material cannot be seen through. Most scrapbooking papers and cardstock are opaque.

1   This three-dimensional layout is based on a 21.5 x 27 cm (8½ x 11 in) standard page; however, due to the thickness of the layout the cardstock needs to be trimmed by at least 13 mm (½ in) on all sides so that it fits into a standard page protector. Cut foam core board into 13 mm (½ in) wide strips to form the basis of the frame. Double up the strips to increase the depth.

2   Cut a frame about 2 cm (¾ in) wide from the same colour cardstock as you will use for the background. Use strong glue or adhesive tape to attach the foam core to the edges of the background cardstock to create the base.

3   Mount the synthetic grass on the background. Position the photograph next to the grass, using a layer of foam core to raise it to the level of the grass mat. Adhere a transparency printed with the title and journalling to the top of the foam-core frame using double-sided adhesive, then adhere the frame over the top. Apply any finishing touches.

1 Trim the polypropylene sheet to a standard scrapbook page size, in this case 21.5 x 27 cm (8½ x 11 in), and spray with a fixative spray on both sides. Embellish the background with acrylic paints (dye and pigment inks may not adhere to the plastic surface).

2 Print the photograph on an adhesive transparency and apply to the polypropylene. An ordinary transparency may be used with vellum adhesive spray, if you wish. Spray with a fixative to protect the image.

3 Stamp a stitched tin tile with paint. Add alphabet charms coloured with coordinating paint. Attach the charms to the tile with adhesive dots and attach the tile to the page using the same dots.

OTHER NON-OPAQUE MATERIALS TO USE

- Exposed camera film
- A CD with the silver peeled off
- Moulded plastic packaging from small items (for shaker boxes)
- Sheer fabric such as organdie or chiffon
- Packing tape (see page 24)
- Microscope slides
- Watch glasses
- Glass paints (use on transparencies)
- Glass pebbles

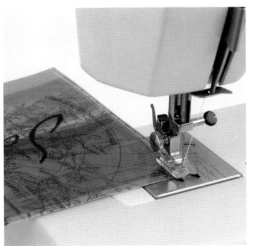

1 Create a layered effect by printing photographs and journalling on transparencies and overlaying the images. Print a beach photograph in colour on textured cardstock as a background. Print a black-and-white photograph (in this example, a shipwreck) on a transparency and trim them both to the same size, so that the shipwreck appears to be in the water of the background photograph.

2 Use a preprinted transparency or print your own transparency with an evocative word and trim it to fit the images. Assemble the layers and machine stitch along one edge of the booklet. This binds the pages together and enables the reader to view the images and words separately by turning the pages.

3 Glue the booklet to the centre of the page. To make the cover, use a craft knife to cut a rectangular opening in a piece of cardstock so that the images can be seen through the cover. Tear and ink around the outside edges to give a weathered feel. Place the cover over the stitched booklet and secure the cover through all layers, with eyelets or decorative brads.

MINI MEMORY ALBUM

Enclose a handmade mini album in a decorated tin case to preserve special family memories. Photographs, tiny tags with quotations and memorable sayings or personal journalling and tiny embellishments make this miniature memento a treasure indeed and a true family heirloom.

CONSTRUCTION

The cover for a mini album can be cut from the same weight of cardstock as the pages, or you can use a heavy card and cover it with fabric or paper to give a more elegant finish. Remember to think about your method of fastening the pages and covers together and allow space for the fastenings. Punch holes for jump rings or ribbon, or use acid-free adhesive tape. You might prefer to sling the pages of the mini album on a single ring at the top left-hand corner.

Fastenings need to be sturdy as each opening of the pages results in wear and tear on the hinge or tie, so consider how often the album is likely to be handled when deciding on a fastening system. If you are going to reinforce holes with eyelets you will need to consider the thickness of the eyelets when deciding on the number of pages for the mini album.

MINI ALBUMS

Made for any occasion or for no occasion at all, a mini album is an ideal gift. The compact nature of a mini album means it is easy to store, especially for someone who does not normally keep a bookshelf full of scrapbook albums. For Mother's Day or Father's Day it is a thoughtful gift that will be much appreciated for the care and creativity that go into it as well as the love that it expresses. Other occasions that could be celebrated in specially constructed mini albums include birthdays, anniversaries, holidays and weddings.

Creating your own custom-sized mini albums is not difficult, although books with ready-made pages, covers and bindings are often available at scrapbook supply stores.

If you want to enclose the mini album in a specific container such as this business card tin, simply make an album to fit the container. Adjust the measurements of the pages to the size of the container and create as many pages as you need to make the album the correct thickness. Remember to leave some room for embellishments such as metal plaques, fibres and even extra layers of cardstock.

Some may own castles on the banks of the Rhine, and hire orchestras each morning at nine. But richer than I they will never be... I had a dad who spent time with me.
—D. Morgan

treasure

I love Dad

ALYS

greater thing is
there   human souls
         that they

fond memories

Embellish the interior pages of the album with photographs and accents, trying to keep the accents reasonably two-dimensional so the tiny pages will close comfortably. The accents in this album are rub-on words, but bigger album pages can take thicker embellishments such as eyelets, brads, fibres and stickers. Punch two holes on the left hand side of the front of the covers and each page, ensuring that the holes line up exactly, then use jump rings to link the album together.

1 Cut rectangles from cardstock: here the rectangles are 7.5 x 12 cm (3 x 4 in). This mini album has five pages all together, two covers (brown cardstock) and three internal pages (green cardstock). Score across the shorter axis and fold each rectangle in half, creating five 6 x 7.5 cm (2 x 3 in) double-sided pages.

2 Use narrow double-sided adhesive tape to join the folded pages together along the bottom and side edges to create pockets. Use a circle punch to remove a semicircle of cardstock from the top edges of the interior pages so that it is easier to access the tags that will be inserted in them. Brush sepia ink around the edges of the pages, including around the indent.

3 Cover the outside front and back covers of the mini album with patterned paper. Add a title to the front cover using the lettering method of your choice, such as rub-on letters or words.

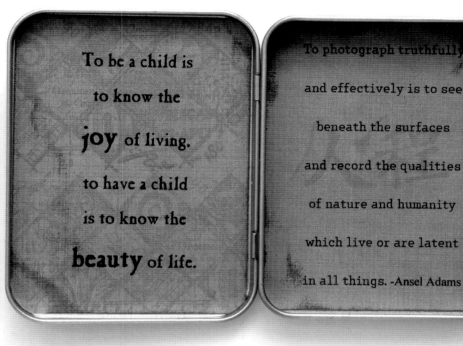

QUOTABLE QUOTES

When using quotations on your scrapbook pages, it's important to properly acknowledge the author and your source. Record the details of the quotation on the reverse of the page.

While you are unlikely to be sued for plagiarism by using someone else's original thoughts in a scrapbook album that is for your private use, it's useful for yourself and for future viewers of the album to be able to attribute a quotation correctly.

The information you need to record is: the person who said or wrote the quotation; the date it was spoken or published; details of the form in which it first appeared (the title and publisher of the book, for example). You should also record your source, whether it is from the original publication or from an anthology of quotes or poetry.

4 Create tags by cutting strips of cardstock to fit inside the page pockets (allow for the double-sided adhesive tape that holds the pockets together). The tags for this size album are 4.5 x 7 cm (1¾ x 2¾ in). Print quotations or journalling on the cardstock for the tags.

5 To decorate the tin, measure the dimensions or trace around the base of the tin to get the required shape for the cardstock lining. Print poems or quotations on the cardstock and cut it to fit inside the tin base and the lid. Stamp a background design onto the cardstock and attach it to the base and inside lid of the tin with double-sided adhesive tape.

6 The top and bottom surfaces of the tin are covered with adhesive paper that has been printed with a rusty metal effect. Peel off the backing paper and press the adhesive onto the tin, then trim the edge flush using sharp scissors or a craft knife. Glue metal embellishments to the top of the tin lid.

LAYOUT ON CANVAS

Scrapbook pages are like works of art, and there is no reason why you shouldn't create a layout that can be hung on the wall and displayed rather than hidden away in an album. Use a pre-stretched canvas from an art-supply shop as a base to show off your favourite photographs and embellishments... and, of course, your creativity.

BLANK CANVAS

Pre-stretched canvas is readily available in most craft and art-supply shops. It comes in many sizes and shapes.

The texture of the canvas provides interest in the background; however, if you want a smoother look, mix gel medium with your acrylic paint.

If you like the canvas look but don't want the depth of the stretching frame, use unstretched canvas instead.

ADHESIVES

Attach photos and embellishments with strong, acid-free adhesive such as liquid glue, double-sided foam adhesive tape or glue dots. Clear acrylic glazes, such as are used for decoupage, can also be useful when strong liquid adhesive is required.

Eyelets, brads and nailheads can also be set through the canvas.

1 Paint the canvas with gesso using a stiff-bristled paintbrush. This will give a prepared surface for the acrylic paints. Make sure you paint the sides of the canvas and on the back as this piece will not be framed.

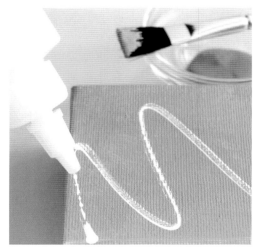

2 Mix acrylic paint to a shade that suits your layout. Paint and allow the background colour to dry completely. Mix flow medium with white acrylic paint in a squeeze bottle with a nozzle (such as an empty glue bottle) and squeeze a decorative swirl over the background. Allow to dry.

3 Use a contrasting colour of acrylic paint to cover decorative foam stamps and stamp the corners of the canvas. When this layer of paint is completely dry, attach photographs and other embellishments.

CHAIN OF POSTCARDS

When you receive postcards from friends and family who have been travelling, it's natural to want to include the wonderful images in a scrapbook layout. However, you also want to be able to read the personal greeting on the reverse of the cards. Here we reveal a novel way of displaying postcards that allows you to view both sides.

1 Lay out the postcards in order and select appropriate fastenings for each pair. For the pair that will be hinged together, place the cards back to back with the bottom edges aligned and place open hinges over the top of the first card. Use an awl to make holes through the hinges into the cards. Separate the cards and use brads to secure the hinges to each card through the holes.

2 To use jump rings, insert eyelets in the adjacent edges of a pair of cards, ensuring that the eyelets are close to the edge of the cards. Open the jump rings and place one through each eyelet, closing the rings again. Link opposite rings with a third jump ring. Use small pliers to open and close the jump rings.

3 For rivets and ribbons, use a suitably sized hole punch to make holes for the rivets, then insert the rivets according to the manufacturer's instructions. Thread 15 cm (6 in) lengths of ribbon through the holes in the rivets and tie in small bows or knots. You can use other methods of fastening the cards together. such as tying them with fine wire threaded through eyelets.

WEARABLE SCRAPBOOKS

Miniature albums made of tags or tiny pages attached to chains, beads or ribbons are wearable art. The size constraints of wearable albums present new challenges, extending your creativity into a new dimension–a tiny one. Wear these small scrapbooks on lanyards and chains, or attach them to key rings, belts and brooches.

ACCESSORIES OF LOVE

The format of a wearable scrapbook could be a tiny booklet, a selection of tags (as shown on this page), a simple locket made of paper and cardstock, or even a single embellished image. You can purchase ready-made wearable scrapbooks which you can decorate yourself, or you can make your own designs for these accessories from your choice of cardstock and paper.

Hang the accessory from a chain, a string of beads, a twisted cord with a tassel, or a shoelace-style lanyard. Add a short chain and a split ring to make a key ring, or a decorative pin to wear it as a brooch.

When these very personal scrapbooks are not being worn, they can be displayed in your home: they look great hanging from the corner of a mirror or a wardrobe doorhandle.

1 For the cover of this wearable scrapbook, take a preprinted, striped paper tag and use abrasive paper to roughen the appearance and expose some of the white core. Decorate with alphabet rub-ons and ink the edges to personalize the design.

2 Use the tag for the cover as a template to cut four more tags from coordinating cardstock, then decorate these tags with photographs, rub-on words, stamps and ink. They form the pages of the wearable scrapbook.

3 Trim photographs to the size of the tags, glue in place and embellish as desired. The edges were roughened with abrasive paper and inked, then rub-on words and phrases were added.

4 Create different forms of embellishment for each tag: use photographs on one, graphic designs or quotations and inspirational words on another. To create a graphic background on plain tags, cover the surface with dark ink then create designs using bleach as shown in the following step.

5 Place a synthetic foam sponge in a container and pour in a small amount of bleach. Use the sponge as an ink pad to apply bleach to a decorative foam stamp. Press the foam stamp onto the inked area of the tag–the bleach will remove the ink, exposing the background paper colour.

ALTERED COMPACT DISC ALBUM

Using altered compact discs for the covers makes a stylish and portable miniature album. Print black-and-white photographs directly onto the cardstock pages, along with memorable quotations. Cut the cover disc with scissors or a craft knife and add hinges, then score the internal pages along the fold line to enable easier browsing.

CRACKLE MEDIUM

There are two types of crackle medium, and both are designed to work with acrylic paints. One is a glaze that you apply over a freshly painted surface. The milky glaze dries clear, producing fine cracks like crazed porcelain. The cracks can be emphasized, if necessary, by rubbing with contrasting coloured chalks or metallic wax-based pigments, or even by painting with a very diluted coat of contrasting acrylic paint.

Another form of crackle medium is applied over a base coat of acrylic paint. When a second coat of paint in the same or a different colour is applied over the crackle medium, the medium prevents it from adhering completely to the base coat. It causes the top coat to crack as it dries, resembling old, flaky paint and revealing the solid colour underneath.

Both effects give an aged appearance to a freshly painted surface, so choose the appearance you prefer.

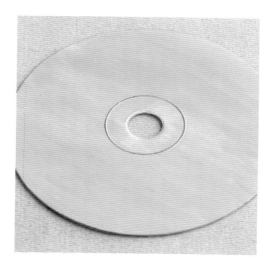

1 Sand the surface of a compact disc with fine abrasive paper to give it some texture and allow the paint to grip. Paint with gold acrylic paint. Allow it to dry, then sand again lightly. Repeat these steps until you have a good, solid coverage of gold paint.

2 Randomly apply crackle medium to the painted surface—the entire surface of the CD does not need to be covered to achieve the effect shown in this project. Allow the medium to become touch dry (depending on thickness of application, temperature and humidity, this could take between five minutes and an hour).

3 Quickly brush white acrylic paint over the crackle medium surface. Use smooth brushstrokes to apply the paint in a single application. Allow to dry. While drying, cracks will begin to appear on the surface, splitting the white paint and allowing the undercoat of gold to show through. Score the CD with a craft knife before cutting to prevent the paint from flaking off.

FRAMED FOR DISPLAY

The best and most creative scrapbook pages deserve to be displayed. A custom-made frame for a special layout is one way to preserve the page; however, ready-made frames, purchased from scrapbook supply stores, mean that you can rotate the display as you choose and constantly create new works of art for your walls.

FRAME FEATURES

A custom-made frame consists of three main parts: frame, mat and glass. The frame is usually made from timber that is painted, gilded or varnished. There is no need to be concerned about the lignin from the timber damaging the scrapbook page as in most custom-made frames the wood will not come into contact with the page itself. If you are concerned, speak to your framer about it.

Most framers will add an acid-free mat board in your choice of colours as a border around the image; however, this is not essential if you feel that your layout has sufficient border area in it already.

Choose a mat—or multiple mats—on the advice of your framer: they will help you with a selection of colours and sizes that complement the scrapbook page. If in doubt, choose white or off-white, as this works with most colour schemes.

The glass in the frame protects your scrapbook page from dust and other environmental elements. You can ask your framer to use UV-filtering glass or Plexiglass for even better protection.

The glass should not touch your scrapbook page. Your framer can add spacers of various thicknesses to accommodate lumpy embellishments. Consider a deep box frame if you have lots of soft, loose embellishments.

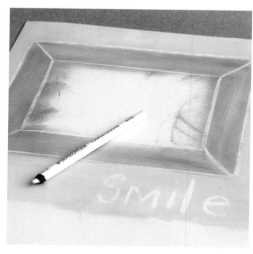

1 Cut a piece of scrap cardstock the same size as your photograph to use as a template. Use a white wax (china marking) pencil to trace around the edges of the template onto glossy white cardstock. (Note that the picture shows blue wax pencil on matte cream stock for clarity only.) Draw a freehand frame around the outline of the picture and add other motifs and words.

2 Apply ink to the frame area as well as to the remainder of the background. Drag an ink pad over the glossy surface, then gently buff the surface with a facial tissue to blend in streaks and soften the colour. Use a heat tool to set the ink on the surface.

3 When the ink is dry and cool, use a clean facial tissue to rub away the wax pencil and the ink adhered to it. Repeat the inking process to fill in any gaps or darken light patches. Then use black ink to emphasize some details. Attach embellishments and the main photograph to the page. Take the page to your framer for a professional finish.

1 This layout has a border as part of the design, so it has been simply placed in a 30.5 x 30.5 cm (12 x 12 in) frame without a mat. The ornate wooden frame complements the gold embossing enamel featured on the layout. Using heat-resistant double-sided adhesive tape, create a border for heat embossing.

2 Sprinkle the tape with ultra-thick embossing enamel and melt the crystals with a heat tool. One layer of enamel gives this slightly textured effect when the melted liquid has cooled.

3 Apply embossing fluid or ink to a wooden letter, ensuring that you cover the whole surface of the letter. Tip embossing enamel crystals into a shallow, flat container and press the inked surface of the letter into the crystals to get an even coverage.

4 Use a heat tool to melt the crystals, then allow the liquid enamel to cool. Repeat this process three times. While the final coat of enamel is still hot, press a script stamp into the melted enamel. (To help prevent the enamel from sticking to the stamp, apply clear embossing fluid to the stamp first.)

5 Use a glue pen or embossing fluid pen to write the title for the page, and cover the fluid with ultra-thick embossing enamel crystals.

6 Use a heat tool to melt the crystals onto the title and allow them to cool. The heart button embellishments on this page have also been created using ultra-thick embossing enamel. Melt enamel with a heat tool in a heatproof container—such as a disposable foil pie tin—and pour the liquid into a decorative heart-shaped mould. Use when cool.

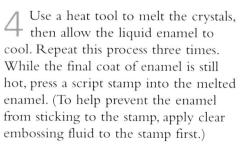

GREETING CARDS AND GIFT TAGS

The papercraft skills you have developed in scrapbooking can be turned to other uses, such as creating unique cards for birthdays, holidays and other special occasions. Using scraps of leftover cardstock and your scrapbooking materials and tools, you can make personalized cards that will be sincerely appreciated by your friends and family.

RESIST TECHNIQUES

Resist painting or dyeing techniques originated with ancient crafts such as batik, the millennia-old Indonesian craft that uses melted wax to paint patterns on fabric before dyeing.

Instead of wax, several different media can be used to create resist designs on cardstock for scrapbooking and paper craft. Wax (china marking) pencils, as on page 92, can be used to write words and draw designs. Children's wax-based crayons also work well as resist media.

The examples on this page have been created using clear embossing fluid and enamel. You can also use repositionable adhesive tape or masking tape to create patterns. Masking liquid (liquid frisket) is a latex formula that can be painted on to make patterns for resist. Resist ink in pad form is also available; it needs to be heat-set before painting over it.

ACRYLIC OR WATERCOLOUR

All paints, including oil paint and tempera paint, are made of pigments (colour) mixed with a binding agent. Acrylic paints use a polymer emulsion binder that dries permanently. Watercolours, on the other hand, are bound with gum Arabic, which is resoluble even after it is dry, allowing the colour to be manipulated simply by using a wet brush.

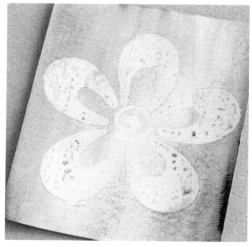

1 Stamp a design onto cardstock using a pad of clear embossing fluid. Sprinkle clear embossing powder over the stamped design, shake off the excess powder, then use a heat tool to melt the powder and set the embossed design on the card.

2 Lightly wet the surface of the design by spritzing with water. Use a soft brush to apply watered-down acrylic paints or watercolours, until the desired effect is achieved. Use a cotton-tipped swab to clean excess paint from the embossed surface. Allow the paint to dry.

3 Place the embossed surface face down on several sheets of scrap paper such as brown paper (make sure they do not have any printing on them as this will transfer to the project). Set an iron to medium-hot and press over the back of the cardstock. The embossing enamel should be absorbed by the brown paper, although you may need to repeat the process a few times.

EMBOSSED METAL

Metal shim can be embossed in the same ways as cardstock or paper. Freehand embossing requires a stylus, a design and a soft mat to allow the impression of the stylus to be made in the metal. You can draw a design freehand or print it on a computer printer. A rubber stamp can also be used to make initial impressions, which can then be sharpened with a stylus. As freehand embossing is done from the reverse of the metal sheet, remember to reverse the design or lettering if there is a definite correct way that it should be seen.

Embossing with a diecut machine or a hand-embossing stencil system makes the job easier. The Zip'e Mate personal diecut machine includes an embossing mat and plate as well as a diecut plate.

A stencil system like the Fiskars ScrapBoss is an alternative method of embossing using double stencil sets. One stencil goes behind the cardstock or shim, the other goes on top. The top stencil is used as a guide for the embossing stylus while the bottom one provides a recess into which to the raised embossing can be pressed. The Fiskars system can be used to emboss areas up to 30.5 x 30.5 cm (12 x 12 in). The designs featured on this page are embossed using the Fiskars ScrapBoss system.

1 Emboss a motif onto medium-weight metal shim, using the method of your choice. A simple motif works best on a small piece of shim for a greeting card or gift tag.

2 Paint the embossed surface all over with a coat of acrylic paint. Allow the paint to dry and repeat the application. Allow to dry thoroughly.

3 Use fine abrasive paper to sand over the painted and embossed surface. Sanding removes the paint, mostly on the raised areas. Continue until the desired level of distressing is achieved. Use a clear sealer or fixative spray, if desired, to protect the finish.

TIME CAPSULE

A time capsule is a container full of items and documents that represent a particular time or date. Traditionally, time capsules were built into the foundations of monuments to be opened in the distant future, but simple time capsules to celebrate one year or a stage in the life of a child can be opened much sooner than that.

SUGGESTED CONTENTS

- Newspaper from the child's birthday (scan and print the front page on acid-free paper)
- DVD or CD with the child's favourite song (perhaps with the child singing the song)
- Photographs of favourite clothing and toys
- Mini books with lists of favourite colours, events, sayings or nicknames
- School photographs and reports
- Stickers and embellishments that represent hobbies and activities
- Letters from special people: parents, family and friends
- A record of physical details: height, weight, shoe size, hair colour

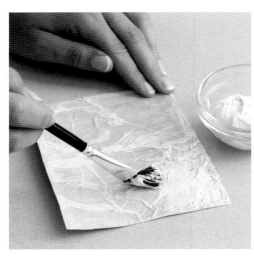

1 Create a distressed leather look for the cover of the time capsule container using this simple method: brush liquid adhesive over the surface of the cardstock or box. Tear strips of tissue paper, scrunch them up and press them onto the surface. Trim away the excess, if necessary, and allow to dry.

2 Brush over the tissue-papered surface with more liquid adhesive, ensuring that all of the paper has adhered to the cardstock. Allow to dry completely. Paint the surface with off-white paint and allow it to dry.

3 Highlight the creases and ridges in the surface with metallic wax-based pigments. Apply with a soft paint brush or use your fingers, if you prefer.

SILVER LEAF ALBUM COVER

Metal leafing turns an ordinary album cover into a precious keepsake. In this example, the silver leaf is applied to adhesive lightly brushed over the surface, emphasizing the embossed pattern. To achieve a traditional gilded effect, apply the adhesive all over the cover and carefully press the metal leaf into the embossed design with a soft paintbrush.

CUSTOM ALBUM COVERS

A handmade cover for an album adds a personal touch. The cover of a mini album for a special occasion will be enhanced by silvering or gilding. In the project on these pages, embossed paper is mounted over a stiff card base and fixed with the central photograph to a background of black cardstock. Pages cut from linen-textured paper are bound with a separate spine strip. Large split pins are used in place of screw-in posts.

EMBOSSING WITH METALLICS

Gilding or silvering is just one way to enhance raised designs on cardstock or paper. You can cover the entire surface as in traditional gilding, or use the metal leaf to accentuate highlights of the textured design.

Embossing powder and enamels can also be used to draw attention to raised designs. Use an embossing fluid marker or a small ink pad to place fluid on the areas you want to highlight. Sprinkle powder or crystals over the surface and shake off the excess. Use a heat tool to melt and set the powder.

Rubbing raised design areas with metallic wax-based pigments is another option, or simply paint them with acrylic paint mixed with metallic pigment powder, such as Pearl Ex. Use a dry brush for more random coverage.

1 Cut embossed paper or cardstock to the size of the album cover and remove a small window from the centre of the cover. Randomly brush white liquid adhesive over the embossed surface and allow it to dry slightly; the glue will become clear and feel tacky.

2 Wear cotton gloves and use your fingers to press silver metal leaf over the surface. Make sure that all of the areas painted with adhesive are covered.

3 Use a firm bristle paintbrush to brush away the leaf that has not adhered to the surface. The brushing also polishes the remaining metal leaf, giving a beautiful, soft shine. Apply a fixative spray or a sealant, if desired.

ALTERED BOOK

This popular style of papercraft uses many of the same skills as scrapbooking. Take on the challenge of creating an altered book as a special project, then transfer some of the new skills you've learned back to your scrapbook album pages.

alter (ôl'tər), **vt. 1.** To make different in details but not in substance; modify. (*Webster's New World College Dictionary*, Third Edition, Macmillan, 1988)

ALTERING BOOKS

Every altered book will be very different and it would be almost impossible to make an exact copy of another book, because of the range of secondhand materials used for each project. Each altered book is therefore an absolutely unique creation.

There are five or six basic steps in altering a book. First, select a strong, well-bound book, usually one with sewn binding. Books with glued binding tend to come undone during the altering process. To find out the type of binding on a book, fold it open so the front cover touches the back. If there is an open arch at the spine, the book is probably sewn. If the pages stick to the spine and the arch is closed, the binding is glued. Another important consideration when choosing your book is the content. You can choose a book that suits your theme and make use of some of the words or illustrations in your artwork, or you can ignore the subject of the book completely.

The adhesive used to stick the groups of pages together will take some time to dry. Place sheets of greaseproof paper in between each of the newly glued page sections, then leave to dry overnight under some very heavy books. When the pages are dry and flat, you can cut windows and niches into the glued pages to display embellishments.

Follow the step-by-step photographs on the following pages to begin altering your selected book.

EQUIPMENT LIST
- Metal ruler
- Cutting mat
- Craft knife
- Paintbrushes
- Eyelet punches and setters
- Wire cutters and pliers
- Scissors
- Sponge daubers
- Pin drill or drill with mini drill bits
- Sponge brushes
- Expired credit card
- Skewers
- Heavy books for flattening
- Heat tool
- Pencils

MATERIALS

You will need:

- A book, preferably with a sewn binding
- Pages from other old books, including sheet music, pages in different languages, dictionaries
- Matchbox
- Faux leaves and flowers
- Cardstock
- Paper: tissue, handmade paper, scrapbooking papers, embossed paper, vellum, faux suede, joss paper, bingo cards, old greeting cards
- Scrap paper for tracing templates
- Tags, precut or cut your own with a stencil
- Brass or metal shim
- Mini metal hinges
- Metal words
- Polymer clay
- Acrylic paints
- Metallic paints and rub-ons
- Letter tiles
- Alphabet rub-ons
- Eyelets
- Coloured art wire
- Beads: seed beads, glass, plastic, wood, shells
- Fancy fibres and yarn
- Metallic thread
- Tiny glass mosaic tiles
- Mirrors
- Trinkets: buttons, old keys, brass charms, rhinestones, old door plates, glass pebbles, old watch parts
- Alphabet stickers and stamps
- Rubber stamps and ink pads
- Adhesives: PVA glue, clear acrylic caulking or sealant, hot glue sticks, double-sided adhesive tape, double-sided foam mounting tape
- Greaseproof paper

1 Altering a book can add a lot of bulk so you will need to remove at least one-quarter of the original pages to make room for the embellishments and additional thickness. Either remove selected pairs of pages at the binding, or place a metal ruler snug against the binding and tear the pages along the edge of the ruler. The second method helps keep the book more intact.

2 The next part of preparing the book is gluing groups of the remaining pages together to make a solid base for niches and embellishments. Use diluted PVA glue and a paintbrush or sponge to apply glue to the front of a page. Close the book and press down on the cover. This prevents pages sticking together on an angle. Allow each glued page to dry a little before gluing the next page.

3 If you are planning to include a niche in the back section of the book, apply the glue only around the edges of the pages. After the glue is dry, trace the shape of the niche onto the book and cut around it with a craft knife. Cut through a few pages at a time and then remove the cut-outs. If you want to include a matchbox drawer, measure it and cut it out.

4 The pages should now be dry, flat and ready to paint. Use acrylic and metallic acrylic paints, as these are fast-drying. Apply paint with different brushes and applicators to achieve different effects. Use a heat tool to dry the paint to touch-dry stage, then place greaseproof paper between the painted sections and leave overnight to dry under a pile of heavy books.

5 Create doors for the niche by gluing together some of the pages that were cut away in Step 4. Trim them slightly after the glue is dry and attach with small hinges. A simple button-and-cord fastening allows them to be opened and closed. A shaped tag booklet can be concealed in the niche.

6 A matchbox becomes a secret drawer, sliding into an opening cut into the section of glued pages at the back of the book. Ensure you leave enough room for the drawer when deciding on the shape and size of the niche. Wire a large bead to the front of the matchbox drawer for a drawer-pull.

WHERE TO GET SUPPLIES

- Craft stores and scrapbooking shops
- Second-hand stores and charity shops
- Junkyards
- Stamping suppliers
- Bead emporiums
- Stationery suppliers
- Supermarkets
- Hardware stores

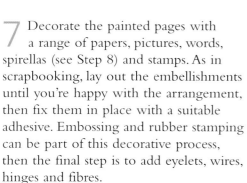

7 Decorate the painted pages with a range of papers, pictures, words, spirellas (see Step 8) and stamps. As in scrapbooking, lay out the embellishments until you're happy with the arrangement, then fix them in place with a suitable adhesive. Embossing and rubber stamping can be part of this decorative process, then the final step is to add eyelets, wires, hinges and fibres.

8 Create a spirella for your book. Trace the shape pictured above, using the template at the back of the book, onto cardstock and cut it out. Tape the end of your thread to the back of the card. Wind the thread around the notches in a clockwise direction until you get back to your starting point. Skipping notches or using different threads can create interesting designs.

7 Wire beads in place for use as handles on drawers, flaps and tags. Cut a length of craft wire about 10 cm (4 in) long. Thread the wire through a seed bead and fold it in half with the bead on the fold. Thread both ends of the craft wire through a large decorative bead and through the cardstock or other material. Separate the ends of the wire at the back of the material and fasten with tape.

TAG BOOK

The book hidden behind the doors
of the niche is a very simple tag book.
Trace and cut out two arch-shaped
pieces of cardstock, one piece of sheet
music and two contrasting pieces of
paper. Use an eyelet for each piece or
for all of them together. Embellish with
images, paint and stamps or stickers.
Thread fibres through the eyelet and tie
on a handmade polymer clay charm.

COVERS

You can use many different materials to
cover your book. You can paint and glue
as in the inside of your book. You can
cover with fabric decorated with beads
or embroidery or use stamps and
embossing powder. Paper and cardstock
cut to size are very simple covers.
This book has been covered with
scrunched-up tissue paper, glued to the
cover with PVA glue, with the edges
folded onto the inside and covered with
a cardstock inside cover. Once the glue is
dry, you can add other embellishments:
the decorations on the front of this book
echo the arch shape of the niche and tag
book, in faux snakeskin fabric, gold
painted sheet music and metal shim.

ONLINE INSPIRATION

For more ideas on altering books,
why not try a search of the Internet?
Simply type the words 'altered
books' into your favourite search
engine and be inspired!

INDEX OF MATERIALS AND TECHNIQUES

PROJECT MAKERS

Thunder Bay Press
An imprint of the Advantage Publishers Group
5880 Oberlin Drive, San Diego, CA 92121-4794
www.thunderbaybooks.com

Editorial Project Manager: Melody Lord
Designer: Michelle Cutler
Photographer: Ian Hofstetter
Stylist: Anne-Maree Unwin
Additional Text: Melody Lord
Scrapbooking Consultants: Ngaire Bartlam, Lynita Chin, Abby Hogarth, Mishell Lancett, Helen Palsson, Tracy Robinson, Barbara Schipplock, Dawn Stan, Helen Williams
Template Design and Illustration: Michelle Cutler and Tracy Loughlin
Production: Monika Paratore

ISBN 1-59223-481-X

Printed by 1010 Printing International Limited.
Printed in CHINA
1 2 3 4 5   09 08 07 06 05

ALPHABET TAGS

A   A   B   B   C

C   D   D   E   E

F   F   G   G   H

H   I   I   J   J

K   K   L   L   M

TRACEABLE ALPHABET

A B C D E F G H I
J K L M N O P Q R
S T U V W X Y Z

A B C D E F G
H I J K L M N
O P Q R S T U
V W X Y Z

ALPHABET TAGS

M N N O O

P P Q R R

S S T T U

U V V W W

X Y Z ? !

MOTIFS

MOTIFS

EMBELLISHMENTS

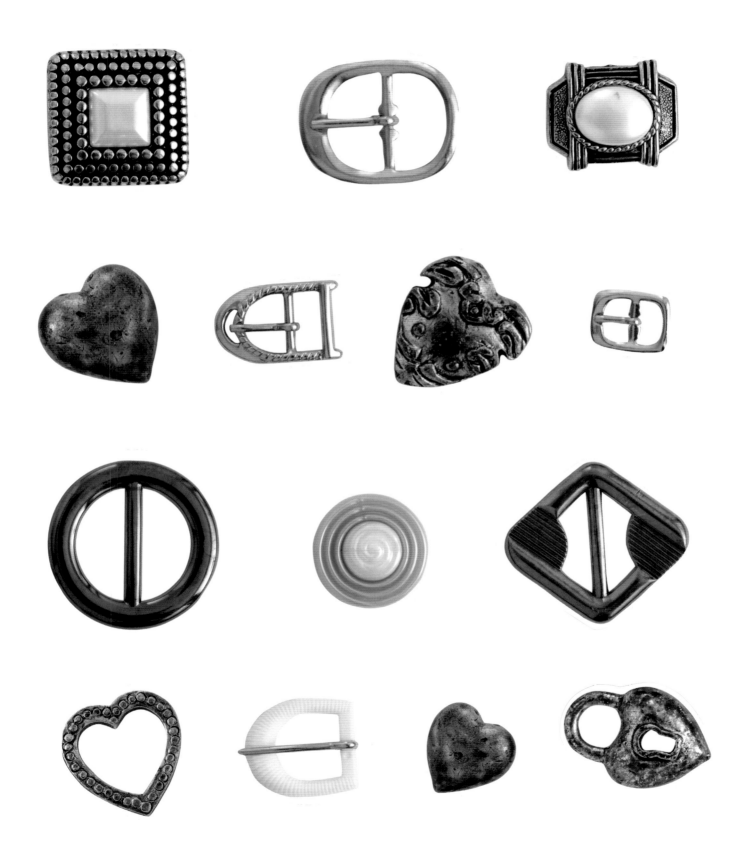

SHELLS

NEGATIVE STRIPS

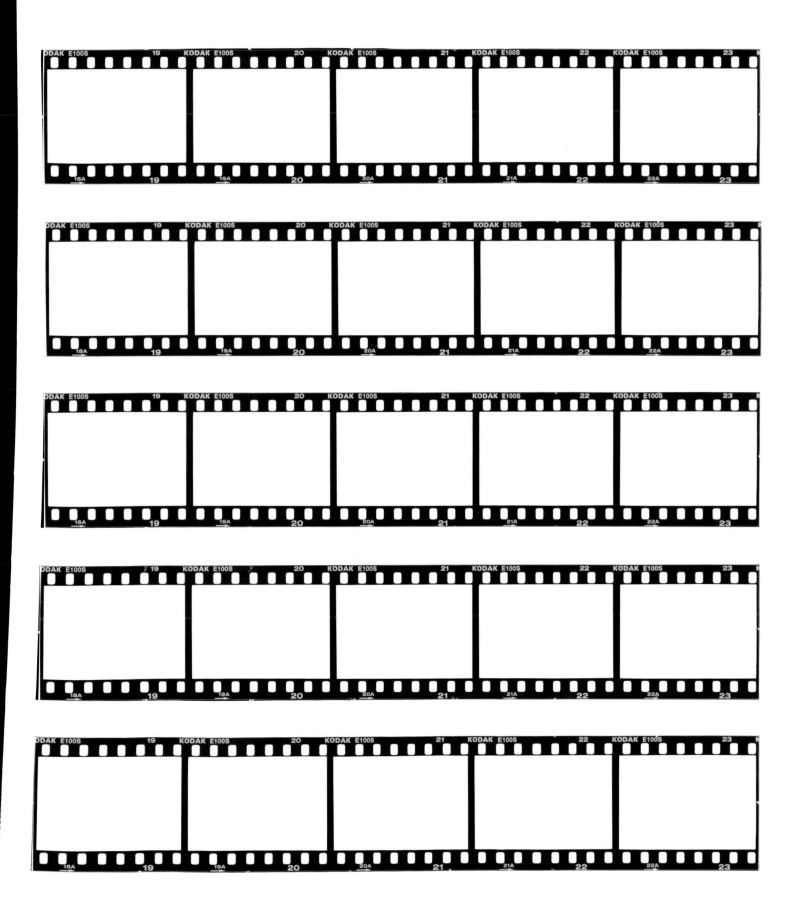

TEXTURES

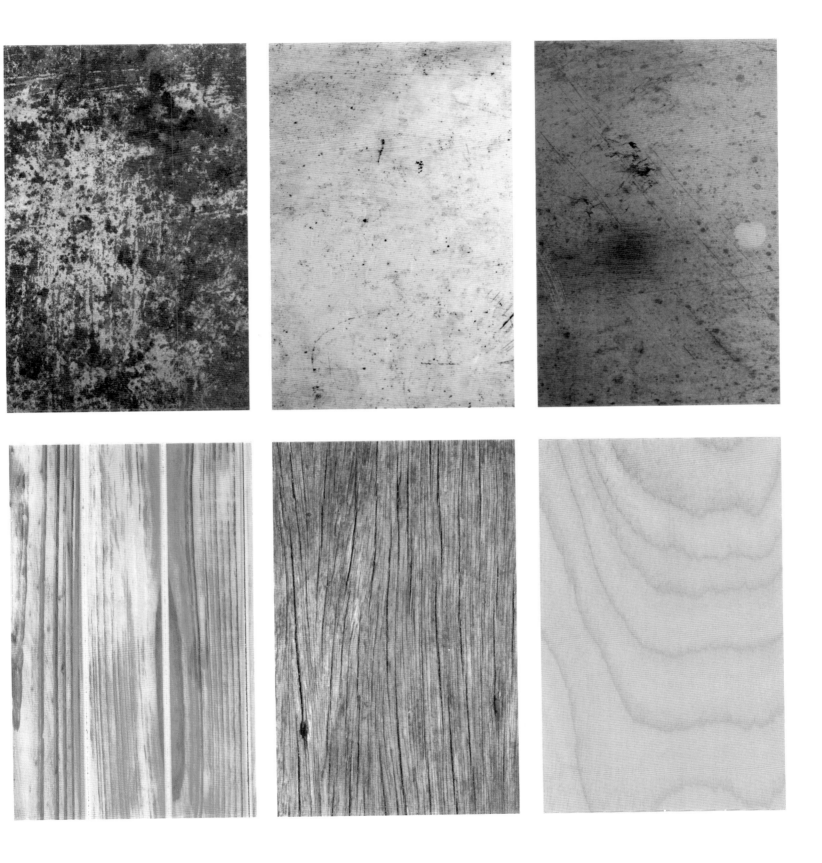

TEXTURES

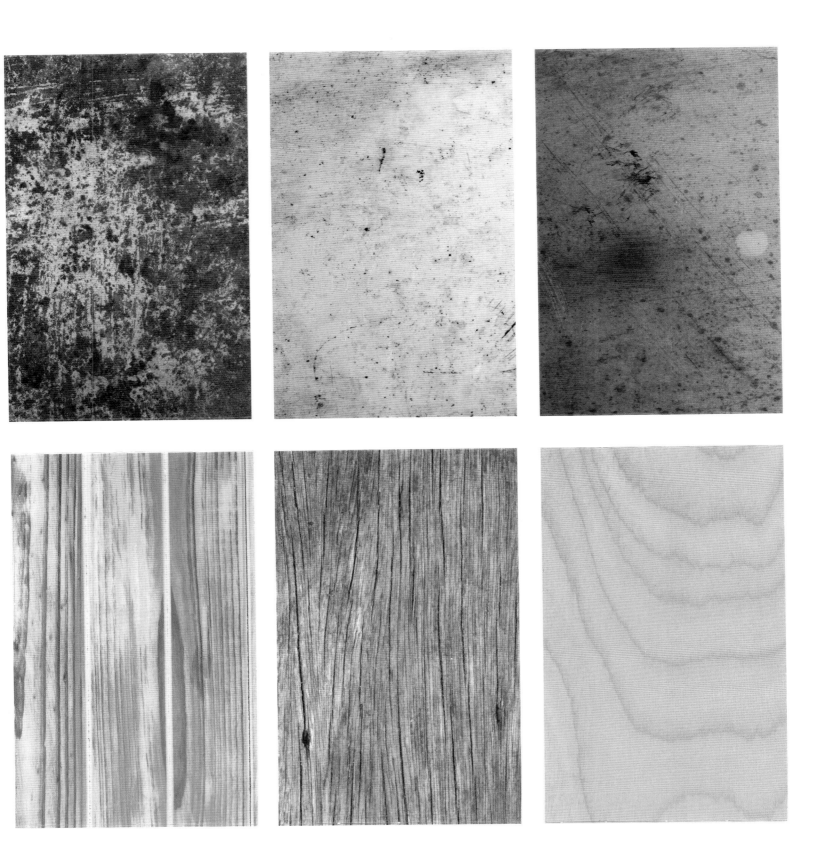

TEXTURES

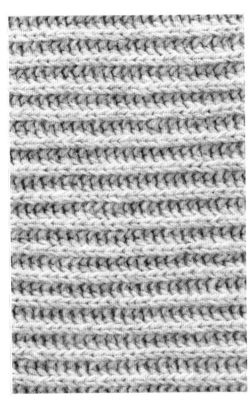

METALS

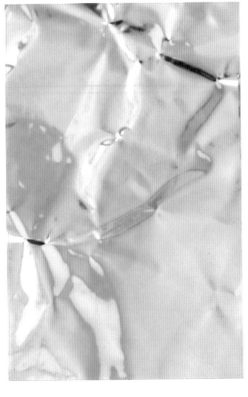

LEAVES

BUTTONS

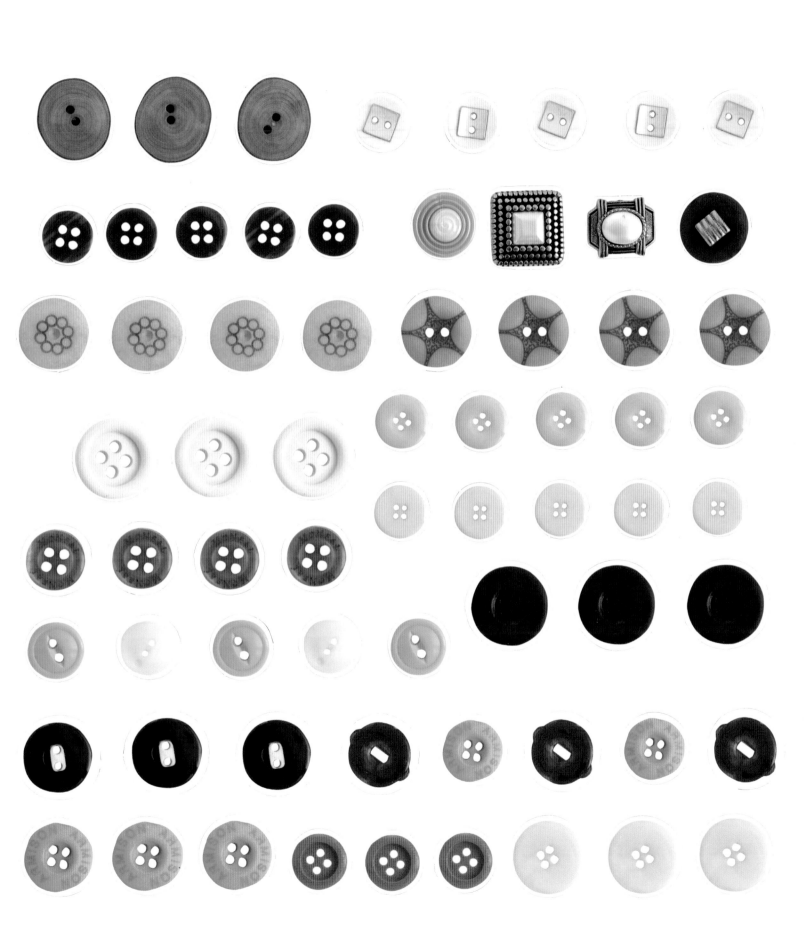

FRAMES

FRAMES

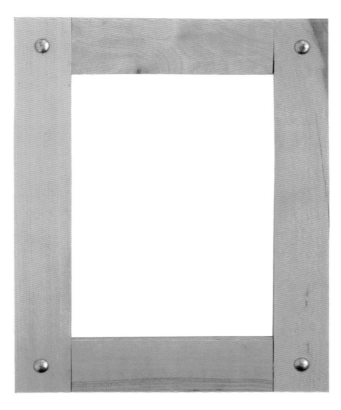

PEBBLES

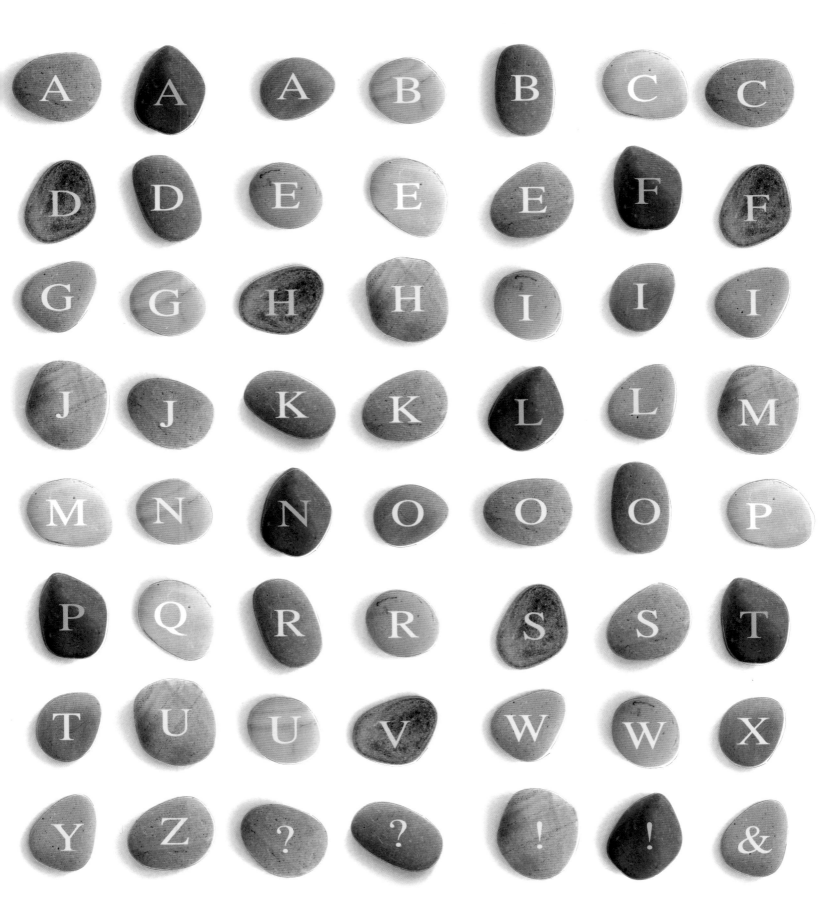

LABEL PLATES

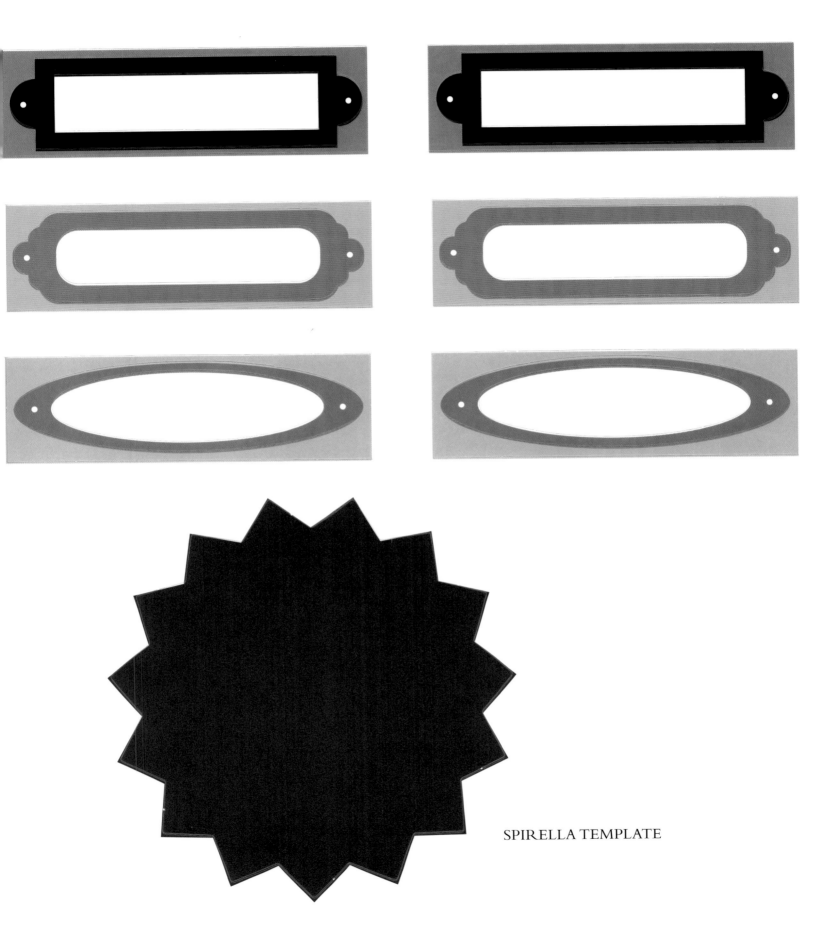

SPIRELLA TEMPLATE

TAGS & REINFORCERS

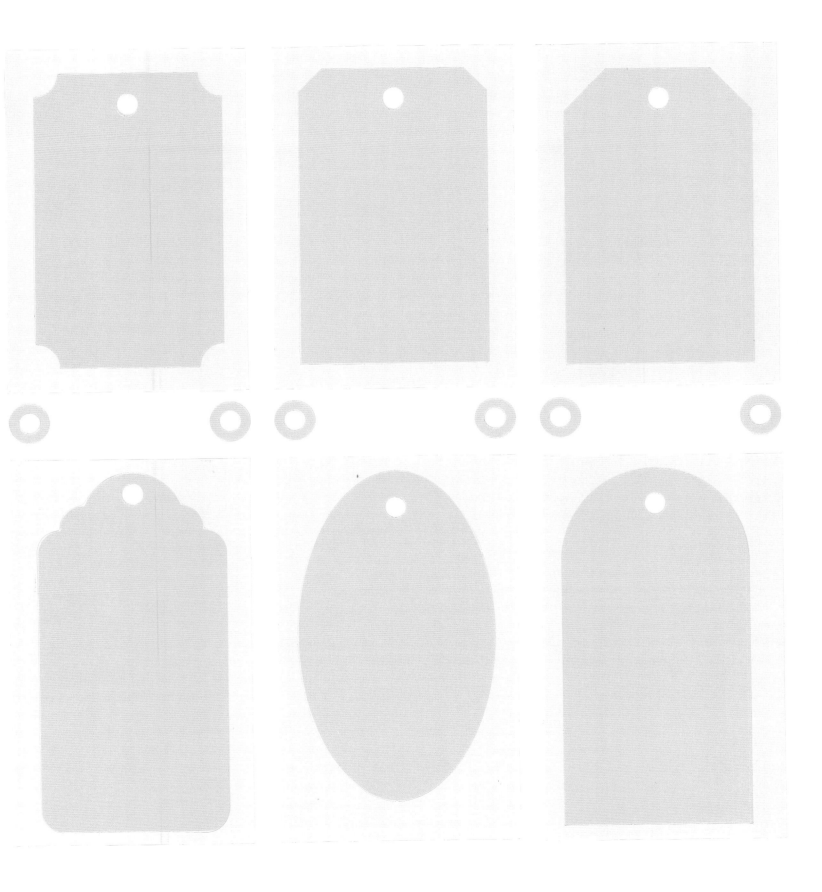

RIBBONS

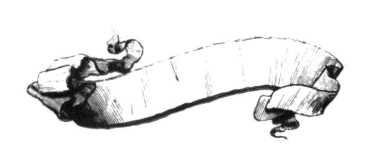

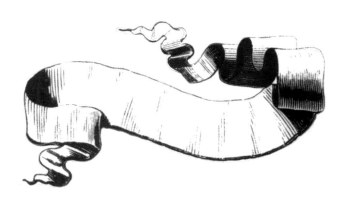

PHOTO CROPPERS

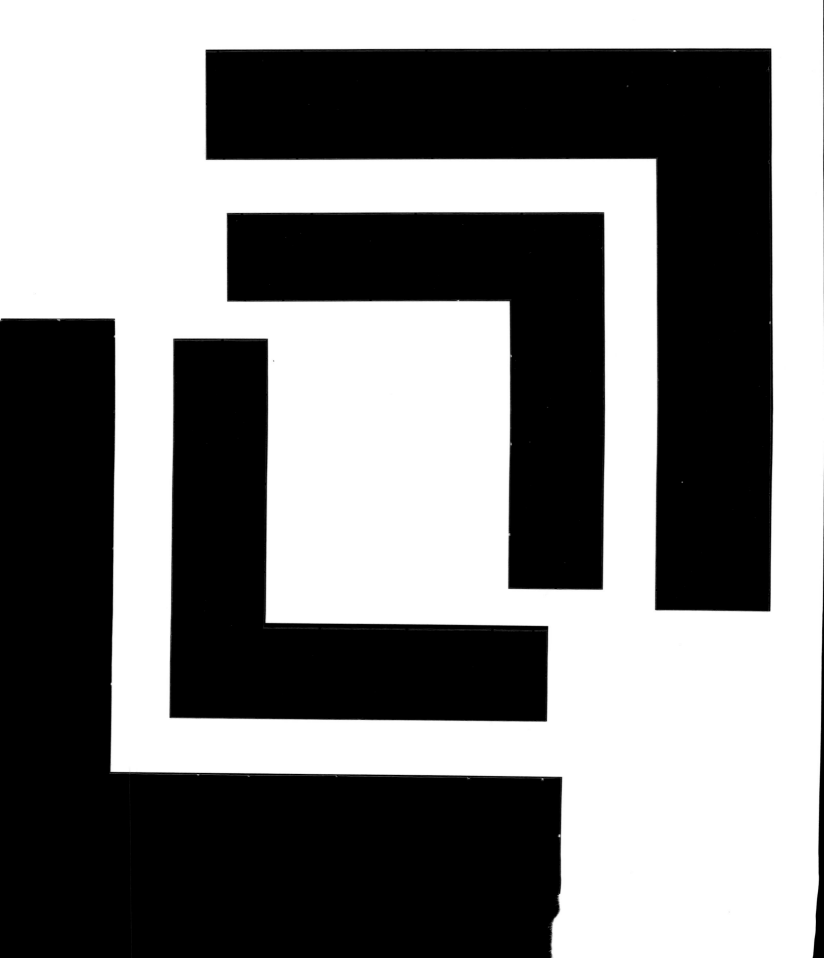